UNDERSTANDING *Capital*

UNDERSTANDING *Capital*

A GUIDE TO VOLUME I

John Fox & William Johnston

PROGRESS BOOKS TORONTO 1978

ISBN 0-919396-39-9

Cover and book design: Danny Hammond

Printing: Eveready Printers, Toronto

Published by Progress Books, 71 Bathurst Street,
Toronto, Ontario, Canada M5V 2P6

Fox, John, 1947-
Understanding Capital

ISBN 0-919396-39-9

1. Marx, Karl, 1818-1883. Das Kapital.
I. Marx, Karl, 1818-1883. Das Kapital.
II. Johnston, William, 1940- III. Title.

HB501.M37F69 335.4'12 C79-094062-0

Contents

Introduction

The present book has grown out of a reading and discussion course on Volume I of *Capital* organized by the Toronto Marxist Institute. The course consists of a number of students reading Volume I for the first time, frequently after unsuccessful attempts at individual study, and is directed by one or two relatively more experienced course leaders.

Why do people gather periodically to work their way through a difficult, century-old text? Some participants are motivated by an intellectual interest in Marxism. Others wish to understand the nature of the economic crisis currently gripping world capitalism and have been unable to find that understanding in so-called "orthodox" economics. Still others are activists who have come to see the limitations of a political practice divorced from a theory of political economy. Members of the women's movement find that material in *Capital* is critical to the current debate over the nature of domestic labour. Labour unionists read *Capital* to understand better the present struggle over wage controls. And so on. One of the most striking developments in contemporary intellectual life is the forceful reassertion of the relevance of Marxian economics after fifty years of relative neglect.

Volume I of *Capital* lays the conceptual foundation for Marx's great work on the political economy of capitalism. The exposition in this volume is careful and logical and, quite apart from its content, the book is a stylistic masterpiece. Yet, the modern reader is likely to find Volume I a difficult book to comprehend, and first attempts to read it often meet with frustration and failure. There are a number of reasons for this common experience.

Capital is firmly grounded in 19th century thought and, therefore, proceeds from an intellectual tradition unfamiliar to most late 20th century readers. At many points in the text, Marx develops or criticizes the ideas of his predecessors and contemporaries.

Furthermore, *Capital* comprises a tight, consistent mental universe. Once that universe is entered, understanding of the text is facilitated, but entry is not usually easily achieved. Part of the difficulty lies in the structure of the exposition in *Capital*, which proceeds generally from the abstract to the concrete (or from higher to lower levels of abstraction), from the fundamental nature of capitalist production to the surface phenomena of capitalism.

Each of us has personal experience with capitalism: with working for wages; with profit and rent; with buying and selling; and with many other aspects of the social and economic system under which we live our daily lives. The ultimate goal of Marx's economic theory is the explanation of these experiences, explanation which serves as a basis for concrete political activity. However, as is common in a scientific endeavour, the explanation is sought not at the level of the experiences, or appearances themselves, but more deeply in the processes and mechanisms which underlie these appearances. It is therefore anomalous that the very familiarity of the surface phenomena of capitalism makes it difficult to probe beneath the surface. Often our direct experiences are so compelling that they dominate our efforts at understanding.

Consequently, a certain patience is demanded of us. Because the general mode of exposition in *Capital* is from the abstract to the concrete, many of the simplifying assumptions made in Volume I are modified and relaxed only later in *Capital*. Volume I of *Capital*, then, starts far below the surface of society. This surface is breached infrequently in the first volume, more frequently in Volumes II and III. The ultimate test of any scientific theory is its ability to account for phenomenal reality. Volume I is the foundation of a theory: its direct test is logical consistency. It is our view, therefore, that in approaching Volume I, the central task is comprehending what Marx has to say and evaluating the logical soundness of his argument. At many points, the theory presented in this first volume is at too high a level of abstraction to warrant direct comparison with reality. We stress, however, that the movement from the abstract theory to the understanding of phenomenal reality is the absolute precondition for the assessment and further development of Marxian political economy. In this regard, recent attempts by British Marxists to come to grips with the nature of the current economic crisis seem to be significant steps in the right direction.

Volume I of *Capital*, then, is a carefully structured work. Therefore, it would appear to be a work which should be read systematically from beginning to end. However, some of the most intellectually demanding material — for precisely the reasons outlined above — occurs in the first three chapters comprising the section on commodities and money. Though grasp of this material is no doubt necessary to a mature understanding of the rest of the book, it is our experience that a first reading is facilitated by encountering the initial section after the rest of the book has been read. We have, therefore, adopted the (unoriginal) strategy of starting with Chapter IV, together with portions of the first chapter which introduce several basic concepts. This approach to the text is motivated by more than expedience. First, the material in the sequel contributes to an understanding of the first section, as well as vice-versa. Secondly, in seeking to comprehend Volume I, the primary task is gaining entry to the structure of the text. At what point that structure is penetrated is in many ways a secondary concern.

Actually, the structure of our book should make it equally suitable for those who wish to read Volume I in its original order. And, in fairness, Marx was aware of the difficulty of the first section of Volume I of *Capital* (see the Preface to the French edition, p. 30), yet he chose not to alter the order of exposition.

The purpose of our book is to encourage individual and group study of Volume I of *Capital*. We hope to assist serious students of Marx through a first reading of Volume I. A mature understanding of this profound text comes only after rereading and further study, but the first reading is critical. It is not our intent to produce a book to be read in lieu of the text, though it may serve that function for certain individuals.

For purposes of the Marxist Institute course, which meets about two hours weekly, Volume I is divided into 11 readings. These readings serve to partition the book into sections of roughly equal length (in terms of reading and discussion time), but they do not correspond to a logical division of the text into parts. Because the division may prove useful to individuals and groups planning to devote effort to Volume I of *Capital* over a period of time, the chapter references for the readings are reproduced below.

Each week of the course, discussion initially centres around a set of questions for that week's reading. We and a number of other individuals have contributed to these questions, a version of which is included in the present book. The general focus of these questions is an understanding of the text.

The main body of our book consists of relatively detailed

summaries of the chapters of Volume I. These summaries seek to abstract the main line of argument in the text and we have generally tried to adhere closely to the original exposition. A minimum of commentary has been included at what we felt to be appropriate places. So as not to distract attention from the main purpose of our book, we have not made reference to the large and growing literature dealing directly or indirectly with Marx's *Capital*. Ideally, the chapter summaries will serve as partial substitutes for, or supplements to, group discussion of the text. We have also included a glossary of terms used in Volume I of *Capital*.

With respect to editions and translations: In preparing this book, we referred to the Progress Publishers edition of Volume I (Moscow) which is based on the Moore and Aveling translation. Quotations and page references, where they occur, are from this edition of *Capital*. A new translation of Volume I by Ben Fowkes (New York: Vintage, 1977) has recently been published. Having read and taught from both translations, it is our opinion that there is little basis for choosing between them.

Finally, we should say a few words about the structure of *Capital* as a whole. The four volumes of *Capital* represent the culmination of Marx's intellectual work. The first volume, concerning itself with the capitalist production process, is of course the subject of the present text. Volume II is devoted to the analysis of the circulation of capital and includes detailed consideration of the circuits, turnover and reproduction of capital. The third volume is subtitled "The Process of Capitalist Production as a Whole." In this volume, Marx extends the theory developed in the first two books, dealing with such topics as the division of profit into components, the laws governing ground rent, the transformation of values into prices, and the formation of a general rate of profit. What was projected by Marx as the last volume of *Capital*, has appeared separately under the title *Theories of Surplus Value*, itself a multivolume work. The three volumes of *Theories of Surplus Value* comprise a critical history of political economic thought.

Of the four volumes of *Capital*, only Volume I was completed by the author and appeared in print during his lifetime. In fact, Marx had the opportunity to reedit this first book on several occasions. Volumes II and III were pieced together by Engels from Marx's extensive notes and drafts. *Theories of Surplus*

Value appeared later under the editorship of Kautsky and, until fairly recently, was unavailable in English.

A careful reading of *Capital* is central to an understanding of Marx's thought. More importantly, grasp of the methods, concepts and analysis presented by Marx in *Capital* is central to an understanding of the political economy of contemporary capitalism and to political activity which proceeds from that understanding. It is, therefore, the task of every student of Marx, and certainly of every Marxist, to come to grips with the material in *Capital*. We hope that our book will assist people in this endeavour.

As we mentioned, several individuals have contributed to the questions included in this text. More generally, we are grateful to students and teachers of the Marxist Institute *Capital* courses and to the members of the Institute collective for their direct and indirect contributions to our efforts. Comments from Rob Albritton, Emil Bjarnason, Bill Carroll, Derek Cooke, Bonnie Fox, and Larry Lyons on an earlier draft are especially appreciated. We should also like to acknowledge the invaluable editorial assistance provided by Mora Gregg and and Maggie Bizzell of Progress Books.

CAPITAL VOLUME I READINGS

1. Chapter I, Section 1 and 2 (pp. 43-53)
   Chapter IV-VI (pp. 145-172)
2. Chapter VII-IX (pp. 173-221)
3. Chapter X (pp. 222-286)
4. Chapter XI-XIV (pp. 287-347)
5. Chapter XV (pp. 351-475)
   Pay particular attention to Sections 1-3
6. Chapter XVI-XXII (pp. 476-528)
7. Chapter XXIII-XXIV (pp. 529-573)
8. Chapter XXV (pp. 574-666)
   Pay particular attention to Sections 1-4
9. Chapter XXVI-XXXIII (pp. 667-724)
10. Chapter I (pp. 43-87)
11. Chapter II-III (pp. 88-144)

CHAPTER I

Commodities

We have seen that when commodities are exchanged, their exchange-value manifests itself as something totally independent of their use-value. . . . The common substance that manifests itself in the exchange-value of commodities, whenever they are exchanged, is their value. (p. 46)

As we noted in the Introduction, we shall delay full consideration of the first three chapters of *Capital* until after the rest of the book has been read. Since at the beginning of Chapter I, Marx introduces several concepts which are essential to an understanding of the remainder of the text, we begin our discussion with the first two sections of Chapter I.

SECTION 1. THE TWO FACTORS OF A COMMODITY: USE-VALUE AND VALUE (THE SUBSTANCE OF VALUE AND THE MAGNITUDE OF VALUE)

It is significant that Marx chooses to open *Capital* with a discussion of commodities. Capitalist production, the primary subject of Volume I, is the generalized production of commodities (although commodity production can take place in non-capitalist contexts as well). By looking first at commodities, Marx begins his investigation of capitalist production with a conceptual microscope. Though he successively broadens its scope, the analysis of commodities remains the foundation of Marx's theory.

Commodities are, first of all, objects. As objects, commodities differ in their concrete properties and, as a consequence of these differences, particular commodities are useful for specific ends or purposes. Commodities as objects satisfy certain human needs and wants. Along with possibly other (e.g., aesthetic) ends, a coat, for example, serves to keep out the cold.

The use to which a commodity may be put is termed its "utility" or "use-value."

Commodities are not, however, merely objects of utility, but useful objects which are the product of human labour. Air, for example, has numerous uses and hence, has use-value or utility, but since it is not a product of human labour, air is not a commodity. Nor is it sufficient for an object to be useful and a product of labour for it to qualify as a commodity. Commodities are products of human labour which are produced in order to be exchanged. Thus, a coat worn by its maker is not a commodity, though a coat acquired through exchange is. Clearly, a product of labour which cannot serve as a use-value for someone other than its producer will not be exchanged and hence is not a commodity. Furthermore, it is possible for objects of utility to be consumed by someone other than their producer without being acquired through exchange. For example, the feudal lord directly appropriates a portion of the product of serfs working on his estates. Since market exchange is not involved, objects appropriated in this manner are not commodities.

Distinct from the use-value of a commodity is what Marx terms its "exchange-value," or the proportions in which the commodity exchanges for other commodities on the market. To illustrate, a coat may be exchanged for a pair of shoes (through barter) or for a quantity of money. Although different commodities are qualitatively different in their use-values, with respect to exchange-value, they differ only quantitatively. The distinction between use-value and exchange-value is fundamental to Marx's analysis. As we shall see, this distinction has manifold consequences and the failure to draw the distinction with clarity is a source of serious confusion and error.

The exchange-value of a commodity is a phenomenal manifestation, or expression, of its "value." That is, we can perceive exchange-values directly by observing the proportions in which commodities exchange for each other on the market. These proportions are not accidental or haphazard; they reflect the relative values of commodities. The distinction between value and exchange-value is not simple to grasp. Marx takes up this distinction in Section 3 of the first chapter, a section to which we shall return later. In any event, for present purposes, we should not lose sight of the fundamental difference between use-value, on the one hand, and value and exchange-value, on the other.

The magnitude of value of commodities is determined by the socially necessary labour time of their production. By "socially necessary" is meant the average time of production under current technological and social conditions. Hence, socially necessary labour time varies with changes in technology, with changes in the skill of the work force, with changes in the social organization of production, with changing social norms regarding the intensity of labour, etc.

Abstracting from certain considerations which Marx deals with later in *Capital* (e.g., supply and demand, capitalist competition), commodities exchange on the market in quantities of equal value. If one coat exchanges for one pair of shoes, it is because the same amount of socially necessary labour time is contained in each. This is the abstract law of exchange of value equivalents, a law which is fundamental to the labour theory of value.

SECTION 2. THE TWO-FOLD CHARACTER OF THE LABOUR EMBODIED IN COMMODITIES

Parallel to the distinction between use-value and value is that which Marx draws between concrete labour and abstract labour. Qualitatively different use-values are produced by qualitatively different sorts of labour: shoes by the labour of the cobbler and clothes by the labour of the tailor. Labour considered in this, its qualitative aspect, is what Marx terms "concrete labour." Concrete labour, therefore, produces particular use-values.

In the production of value, in contrast, labour counts only quantitatively. Since abstraction is made from the particular or concrete character of different sorts of labour, in its role as producer of value, labour is "abstract labour."

Just as different use-values are essentially incommensurable, there are fundamental qualitative differences among the varieties of concrete labour producing these use-values. But in treating the production of value, Marx abstracts from the qualitative differences among the varieties of labour. Value, then, is produced by labour in its abstract or general aspect. And the quantity of value produced is determined by the quantity, measured in time, of labour expended in the productive process.

Not all labour is equally productive. Aside from the range of purely individual differences, more skilled workers produce a greater quantity of use-values of a given sort in a particular amount of time than their less skilled counterparts. Clearly, because of this productivity advantage, the skilled worker produces more value than the unskilled in equal amounts of time. However, there is no difficulty in making quantitative comparisons among the values produced by workers of varying skills (in terms of their relative productivity) and, hence, Marx chooses to make the simplifying assumption that all labour is simple, unskilled, homogeneous human labour, to which all labour, in any event, can be quantitatively reduced.

PART II

The Transformation of Money into Capital

CHAPTER IV

The General Formula for Capital

The value originally advanced, therefore, not only remains intact while in circulation, but adds to itself a surplus-value or expands itself. It is this movement that converts it into capital. (p. 149)

In this and the next two chapters, Marx investigates the transformation of money into capital, value capable of self-expansion. Put another way, he poses and solves the following problem: Where do profits originate? As is typical of Volume I of *Capital*, Marx's argument is rigorously and gradually developed. The argument takes place within the context of the law of exchange of equivalents and against the background of confusion generated by the work of other political economists. In the course of these chapters, Marx solves a problem which perplexed the greatest of the classical economists.

A society of simple commodity producers consists of a number of individuals who satisfy at least some of their needs by exchanging products of their own labour for products of the labour of others. The simple circulation of commodities is symbolized by the "formula" C-M-C, representing the exchange of a commodity for money followed by the subsequent exchange of the money for another commodity (or commodities). For example, a tailor sells clothes that he produces (C-M) and then purchases commodities other than clothes

(M-C) which are necessary for his existence. Since the goal of simple commodity circulation is the realization of use-values, and since these use-values are consumed once they are obtained, the simple circulation of commodities is essentially a self-limiting process. Marx characterizes the circuit C-M-C as "selling in order to buy."

The circuit which characterizes the circulation of capital is not C-M-C but rather M-C-M: the exchange of money for commodities which are subsequently exchanged for money. Marx terms the circuit M-C-M, "buying in order to sell." While the purpose of simple commodity circulation is the realization of use-values, i.e., the satisfaction of wants, the purpose of the circulation of capital is the realization of exchange-value. Of course, the circuit M-C-M would be meaningless if the money realized at its end were no greater than that cast into circulation at its beginning. Hence, the purpose of the circulation of capital is more properly described as the expansion or augmentation of exchange-value. The circulation of money as capital may therefore be described by M-C-M′, which Marx calls the "general formula for capital," where we understand that M′ exceeds M. The difference between M′ and M, the value gained by the capitalist, is called "surplus-value."

Since the circuit M-C-M′ ends as it began, with money, it may be repeated yet another time though, conceivably, on an expanded scale. Thus, unlike the circuit C-M-C, the circulation of money as capital is not a self-limiting process.

CHAPTER V

Contradictions in the General Formula of Capital

Circulation, or the exchange of commodities, begets no value. (p. 161)

Although the formula M-C-M′ characterizes the functioning of capital in the sphere of circulation, it presents problems for further analysis. For if exchange is governed by the law of equivalents, how can the terminal M′ be larger than the initial M?

Attempts to account for profits by assuming a process of exchange in which "both sides gain" confuses use-value with exchange-value. Because an individual exchanges (either directly through barter or indirectly through the agency of money) an object which is not of use to him for one which is, does not imply that the exchange-value of the commodity obtained is greater than that of the commodity parted with.

It is clear that if exchange is governed by the law of equivalents, the circulation of commodities cannot be a source of surplus-value. Furthermore, even if there exists an inherent advantage in selling (or, alternatively, in buying) in the sense that commodities sold draw more than their equivalent in money, this advantage is irrelevant to the realization of surplus-value, since the circuit of capital, M-C-M′ consists of both a purchase and a sale. Thus, for instance, if there is an advantage in buying, any advantage gained in the initial exchange of money for commodities would be lost in the sale of these commodities. Finally, even if particular individuals realize advantages in exchange which do not cancel each other out, no net surplus-value is produced in the transaction, since one individual's gain is another's loss. Here, we witness not the creation of surplus-value in exchange, but the transfer of value from one party to another.

CHAPTER VI

The Buying and Selling of Labour-Power

In order to be able to extract value from the consumption of a commodity, our friend, Moneybags, must be so lucky as to find, within the sphere of circulation, in the market, a commodity, whose use-value possesses the peculiar property of being a source of value, whose actual consumption, therefore, is itself an embodiment of labour, and, consequently, a creation of value. (p. 164)

In the last chapter, Marx demonstrated that if equivalents are exchanged (or even if this rule is consistently or accidentally violated), surplus-value cannot originate in the act of exchange. Consequently, the production of surplus-value is not determined by the values of the commodities entering into the circuit of capital. We are led to the apparently enigmatic conclusion that the production of surplus-value is a function of the concrete properties — i.e., the use-value — of some commodity or commodities which are purchased by capital. What is needed to resolve the contradictions in the formula of capital is a commodity (that the capitalist can purchase) whose use entails the creation of value. Value is created by labour. So, a commodity which is employed to create value must have labour as its use-value. Labour-power, or the capacity to work, is such a commodity.

On first consideration, the distinction between labour-power (the commodity) and labour (the use-value of labour-power) appears somewhat forced and overdrawn. However, as we shall see, this distinction allows Marx to derive a theory of wages and surplus-value consistent with the principle of exchange of equivalents. Indeed, the failure of the classical political economists to draw this or a similar distinction led to inconsistencies in their theories.

In order for a potential capitalist (that is, an owner of money which is to function as capital) to purchase labour-power, two conditions must be satisfied. First, labour-power must exist as a commodity. The potential worker must own his labour-power and be free to dispose of it in the same manner as the owner of any commodity is free to sell it on the market. Secondly, the worker must own only his labour-power and not the means of production with which his labour-power can be combined in the production of commodities. For if a person owns means of production which can be transformed into commodities through his labour, he has the option of being an independent commodity producer rather than a wage-labourer. The existence of a class of potential labourers is the product of historical forces which Marx describes in Part VIII of the first volume of *Capital.*

We mentioned that the introduction of the commodity, labour-power, permits Marx to develop a theory of wages and surplus-value which is consistent with the labour theory of value. Like every other commodity, labour-power has both a value and a use-value. Its value, like the value of all commodities, is determined by the socially necessary labour time entailed in its production. Since labour-power is the labourer's capacity to work, the labour time for the production of labour-power is the socially necessary labour time incorporated in the labourer's subsistence. The labourer's subsistence includes something more than the goods necessary to keep the worker barely alive. Rather, it incorporates all commodities which are required for the production and reproduction of the worker's labour-power including the satisfaction of his "normal" needs, those of his family (since the worker's family is necessary to his existence as well as to the reproduction of the working class), and whatever education and training is required by his job. Therefore, the value of labour-power, determined by the value of the means of subsistence of the worker, is not an immutable quantity. It will vary with variations in the value of these means of subsistence, caused, for example, by changes in productivity of industries producing subsistence goods. More subtly, the value of labour-power will change as the social definition of subsistence changes. This is what Marx means when he says that "there enters into the determination of the value of labour-power a historical and moral element." (p. 168)

Although labour-power is a "peculiar" commodity, it is a

commodity nonetheless. After the capitalist purchases the commodity labour-power, he wishes to use it. Since the use-value of labour-power is labour itself, labour-power is used in the sphere of production, that is, in the creation of new commodities. Hence, like all commodities, labour-power is used, or consumed, outside of the sphere of circulation. In fact, Volume I of *Capital* is almost wholly absorbed in a consideration of the capitalist process of production.

PART III

The Production of Absolute Surplus-Value

CHAPTER VII

The Labour-Process and the Process of Producing Surplus-Value

> *The process of production, considered on the one hand as the unity of the labour-process and the process of creating value, is production of commodities; considered on the other hand as the unity of the labour-process and the process of producing surplus-value, it is the capitalist process of production, or capitalist production of commodities. (p. 191)*

SECTION 1. THE LABOUR-PROCESS OR THE PRODUCTION OF USE-VALUES

In the third part of *Capital*, Marx pursues the consequences of the labour theory of value for the determination of the values of commodities and for the exploitation of workers by capitalists. This discussion begins with a consideration of the production of use-values, what Marx terms the "labour-process."

The production of objects of utility through labour is intrinsic to human existence and, hence, is not specific to particular economic formations such as capitalism. Therefore, the production of use-values ultimately resolves itself into an exchange between man and nature. Throughout *Capital,* Marx differentiates abstract factors and processes which characterize economic activity generally from the specific forms which are characteristic of certain economic formations. An understanding of the specific form of the labour-process under capitalism is facilitated by prior consideration of the labour-process in the abstract.

There are three elementary factors which comprise the labour-process. The first factor is the activity of the worker directed toward the production of a useful article. Secondly, there is the subject of that activity, which may be a use-value provided directly by nature or one which is the product of previous human labour. In the latter event, the subject of labour is termed "raw material." The third factor of the labour-process consists of the instruments of labour, those objects which intervene between the activity of the labourer and the subject of his work. Narrowly construed, the instruments of labour are tools employed in the labour-process. More broadly, they include articles such as buildings which are necessary to, or facilitate, the labour-process. Clearly, the product of one labour-process can serve as raw material or instruments of labour for another such process.

While the general nature of the labour-process is common to all modes of production, it is characteristic of capitalism as a specific mode of production that the labour-process is carried out under the supervision of the capitalist and that the product produced, along with the factors entering into its production, is the property of the capitalist.

SECTION 2. THE PRODUCTION OF SURPLUS-VALUE

Just as a commodity can be viewed as a particular use-value or as a repository of value, the productive process may be considered from the aspect of the production of a particular use-value or from the aspect of the production of value. We have seen how the three factors of the labour-process are common to all modes of social production. It remains to be specified how, under capitalism, these factors enter into the determination of the value of a commodity product.

The value of a commodity is the socially necessary labour time expended in its production. Since certain of the use-values employed in the production of a commodity are themselves commodities, that is products of human labour, the labour expended in their production must also count toward the socially necessary labour time for the production of the product. Therefore, if the raw material used in the production of a particular commodity was the product of six hours of labour, these six hours are included in the socially necessary labour time for producing the commodity, even though they were not expended in the final stage of production.

Similarly, the instruments of production, insofar as they are the products of human labour, enter into the determination of the value of the product. However, since the instruments of labour are consumed only gradually in production, they transfer their value to the product piecemeal as they wear away. If a tool requiring 100 hours of labour for its production is in turn used in the production of 100 articles of a particular sort, it transfers 1/100 of its value to each article or adds one hour of labour time to each.

Of course, the labour directly expended in the production of a particular commodity also contributes to the value of that commodity, and herein lies the secret of the production of surplus-value. The capitalist pays for all of the factors of production at their value. Since the instruments of production and the raw materials employed in the production process merely transfer their value to the product, they are not the source of surplus-value. Labour-power, on the other hand, once purchased, is used as labour. The value of labour-power is a fixed quantity (at a particular point in time) depending upon the value of the means of subsistence of the labourer. The labour which is the use-value of the commodity labour-power, however, creates value in proportion to its duration. And there is no constraint that the daily value of labour-power be equal to the value that labour creates in a day's work.

Suppose, for example, that the subsistence goods required by the worker and his family each day are the product of six hours' labour and, hence, that the worker's daily wage is the money equivalent of six hours of labour. In the first six hours of the working day, the labourer creates new value equal to his wage. If the working day were to terminate after six hours, the value of the product would be equal to the values of the factors entering into the labour-process and no surplus-value would be produced for the capitalist. Alternatively, if the working day extends beyond six hours, the value created by the labourer exceeds the value of his labour-power, realized by the worker as his wage. Hence, the production of surplus-value under capitalism is nothing more than the prolongation of labour beyond the time necessary to reproduce the value of labour-power.

We should note that the distinction between the commodity labour-power and its use-value, labour, allows Marx to account for the production of surplus-value within the labour theory of value and the principle of exchange of equivalents.

CHAPTER VIII

Constant Capital and Variable Capitol

> *That part of capital then, which is represented by the means of production, by the raw material, auxiliary material and the instruments of labour, does not, in the process of production, undergo any quantitative alteration of value . . . . On the other hand, that part of capital, represented by labour-power, does, in the process of production, undergo an alteration of value. (p. 202)*

We have seen how Marx analyzed the labour-process into its several factors. In commodity production, these factors enter differently into the determination of the value of a product.

The value of the means of production, consisting of raw materials, auxiliary materials (items consumed wholly in production but which do not enter into the formation of the substance of the product) and instruments of labour, is simply transferred to the product as the means of production are used up. Since raw and auxiliary materials are wholly consumed in production, all of their value reappears in the product, while instruments of labour, which are consumed gradually, transfer their value piecemeal in proportion as their use-value is worn away. On the other hand, labour which is expended directly in the process of production creates new value which is incorporated in the product.

Marx's earlier distinction between concrete and abstract labour reappears in his discussion of the formation of the value of commodities. Although the point he makes appears to be elusive, it is actually not complex. Labour employed in the productive process serves not only to create new value but also to transfer the value of the means of production to the product. In its role as a creator of value, labour is construed quantitatively in terms of labour time (i.e., as abstract labour). In its role as a transferer of value from the means of production to the product, labour is considered qualitatively as labour of a particular sort (concrete labour). For example, in the construction of shoes, the value of the leather, thread, dye, needles, etc., which are consumed in the production of shoes, is incorporated in the commodity produced. In order to transform these particular means of production into shoes, labour of a particular sort is required, the labour of a shoemaker. A butcher couldn't effect this transformation. However, the value added to the shoes by the labour of shoemaking (as distinct from the value transferred from the means of production) is a function of the labour time expended in the production of the shoes and, as such, is comparable to the labour time expended in butchering.

Since the capital advanced for the purchase of means of production simply transfers its value to the product without undergoing a change in its magnitude, Marx terms this portion of capital "constant capital." In contrast, the capital advanced for labour-power enters through labour into the creation of value. To the extent that labour time extends beyond the time necessary for the replacement of the value of labour-power, surplus-value is created. Because the capital advanced for labour-power can expand its value in the process of production, Marx calls this component of capital "variable capital."

CHAPTER IX

The Rate of Surplus-Value

The rate of surplus-value is therefore an exact expression for the degree of exploitation of labour-power by capital, or of the labourer by the capitalist. (p. 209)

SECTION 1. THE DEGREE OF EXPLOITATION OF LABOUR-POWER

On first reading, Chapter IX may appear to be a confusing kaleidoscope of figures, symbols, and definitions. Upon closer examination, however, the material presented in this chapter resolves itself into formalization, extension and illustration of the topics discussed in previous sections.

We have already seen that the capital advanced by the capitalist for production (represented by the symbol C) is divided into two parts: the value of means of production consumed in the productive process, or constant capital (c), and the value of labour-power, or variable capital (v). The value of the product (C') consists of the value transferred from the means of production (c) plus the value created by the expenditure of labour in the productive process. For surplus-value (s) to be produced, the value created must exceed the value of labour-power (i.e., variable capital). Thus, we have the equation $s=C'-C$. Substituting $c+v$ for C and rearranging the equation, we obtain $C'=c+v+s$. In other words, the value of the product is the sum of constant capital, variable capital and surplus-value.

The value created in the process of production is purely a function of variable capital, since the value of constant capital is merely transferred from the means of production to the product. Hence, Marx distinguishes between the value of the product ($C'=c+v+s$) and the value-product or value created in production ($v+s$). The degree to which variable capital expands its value in the process of production is measured by the ratio of surplus-value to variable capital, s/v, which is termed the "rate of surplus-value." In contrast, the ratio of surplus-value to the total advanced capital, s/C or $s/(c+v)$, is called the "rate of profit."

In Volume I of *Capital,* Marx ignores the rate of profit and develops his analysis exclusively in terms of the rate of surplus-value. There are three essential reasons for this choice. First, as we have noted, constant capital doesn't enter into the production of new value and, hence, its consideration in the present context can obscure the fundamental process of the production of value under capitalism. Secondly, as we shall see presently, the rate of surplus-value is directly interpretable as the degree of exploitation of labour by capital. Finally, although surplus-value originates in the sphere of production, profit is realized only in circulation, through the sale of commodities that have previously been produced. Surplus-value, then, is fundamental in the following sense (among others): the realization of profit is dependent upon the production of surplus-value. As we have mentioned, Volume I deals almost exclusively with the sphere of production. This is not to say that a consideration of circulation and of profit is unimportant to the analysis of capitalism, only that the consideration of production and surplus-value is more fundamental. Marx pursues the analysis of the circulation of capital in Volume II; the concept of profit is dealt with at length in Volume III of *Capital*.

During part of the working day, the labourer reproduces or replaces the value of labour-power, that is, variable capital. During this time, the worker is labouring for himself in the sense that he produces value equal to that of his subsistence, the equivalent of which he obtains from the capitalist in the form of wages. The remainder of the workday is devoted to the production of surplus-value. If the first period of time is termed "necessary labour" and the second "surplus labour," the ratio of surplus to necessary labour expresses the extent to which the labourer is exploited by the capitalist. This ratio, in turn, is equal to s/v, or the rate of surplus-value.

The example presented by Marx on pp. 210-211 is shown in Table 1. Examining this table, we can see that the total capital advanced ($C=430$) is composed of 378 constant capital (c) and 52 variable capital (v), and that the value of the product (C') is equal to 510. Therefore, surplus-value is $s = C'-C = 510\text{-}430 = 80$; the value created is $v+s = 52+80 = 132$; the value transferred is $c = 378$; and the rate of surplus-value is

$s/v = 80/52 = 1.538$ or 153.8%. Of the value created, $v/(s+v) = 52/(80+52) = .394$ or 39.4% represents variable capital, and $s/(s+v) = 80/(80+52) = .606$ or 60.6% represents surplus-value. Therefore, in a 10-hour working day, $10 \times .394 = 3.94$ hours are necessary labour, while $10 \times .606 = 6.06$ hours are surplus labour.

TABLE 1
FORMATION OF THE VALUE OF A PRODUCT
MARX'S EXAMPLE

Commodity	*Symbol*	*Value*		
I. Capital Advanced	C	430		
A. Constant Capital	c		378	
1. raw material cotton (including waste)				342
2. instruments of labour wear on machinery				20
3. auxiliary materials				
a. coal				4.5
b. gas				1
c. oil, etc.				4.5
4. rent				6
B. Variable Capital wages for labour-power	v		52	
II. Product yarn	C′	510		

SECTION 2. THE REPRESENTATION OF THE COMPONENTS OF THE VALUE OF THE PRODUCT BY CORRESPONDING PROPORTIONAL PARTS OF THE PRODUCT ITSELF
SECTION 4. SURPLUS-PRODUCE

Just as the value of the product can be decomposed into constant and variable capital and surplus-value ($C'=c+v+s$), so can the product itself be represented in a similar manner since the materialization of the value of the product is the product itself. The example shown in Table 2 is presented by Marx on pp. 212-215. Of the total value of the product, $C'=30$: $c=24$ or 80% is the value transferred from the means of production; $v=3$ or 10% represents variable capital; and $s=3$ or 10% represents surplus-value. Hence, 80% of the product, or 16 of the 20 lbs. of yarn, corresponds to the constant capital, 2 lbs. to variable capital, and 2 lbs. to surplus-value. The portion of the product representing surplus-value is termed "surplus-produce."

TABLE 2
REPRESENTATION OF THE COMPONENTS OF THE VALUE OF THE PRODUCT BY CORRESPONDING PROPORTIONAL PARTS . . .

(A) COMPONENTS OF THE VALUE OF THE PRODUCT

Component	*Symbol*	*Value*		*Proportion of Value of Product*	
I. Constant Capital	c	24		.800	
A. cotton			20		.667
B. other			4		.133
II. Variable Capital	v	3		.100	
III. Surplus-Value	s	3		.100	
Product 20 lbs. yarn	C′	30		1.000	

(B) . . . OF THE PRODUCT ITSELF

Component	*lbs. of Yarn*	
I. c	16.00	
A. cotton		13.33
B. other		2.67
II. v	2.00	
III. s (surplus-produce)	2.00	
C′ (total)	20.00	

(C) . . . OF THE WORKING DAY

Component	*Time*	
I. c	9.6h = 9h 36m	
A. cotton		8h
B. other		1.6h = 1h 36m
II. v	1.2h = 1h 12m	
III. s	1.2h = 1h 12m	
C′ (total)	12h	

A similar division of the working day into three components is easily calculated. These calculations for Marx's example of a working day of 12 hours are shown in the last panel of Table 2. However, this representation should not be confused with the division of the working day into necessary and surplus labour. Such a confusion can lead to absurd consequences, as we shall see in a moment.

Capital is subtitled, "A Critique of Political Economy," and Marx frequently comments on the work of other political economists. He divides these economists into two general categories: the classical political economists, such as Ricardo, for whom Marx holds a great deal of respect (though he is not uncritical of their work); and the "vulgar economists," apologists for the capitalist system, for whom Marx feels nothing but contempt. Nassau Senior is clearly in this latter category.

Since Senior's analysis is confused and Marx's discussion of Senior's calculations a bit complicated, we shall use the example in Table 2 above to illustrate the fallacy in Senior's reasoning. As we have discussed, the last panel in Table 2 shows that of a 12-hour working day, surplus-value is represented by 1 hour and 12 minutes. According to Senior's reasoning, if the working day were reduced from 12 hours to 10, all of the "profit" should disappear. However, Senior fails to note that the value of the constant capital advanced would decrease proportionately with the reduction in the working day, since fewer commodities incorporating means of production would be produced. In the present case, the yarn produced would decrease from 20 lbs. to 20 × (10/12) = 16 2/3 lbs., the value of the product from $C'=30$ to $C'=30 \times (10/12) = 25$, and the constant capital from $c = 24$ to $c = 24 \times (10/12) = 20$. Since the labourer would require the same subsistence working 10 hours as he did working 12, the value of variable capital would be unaltered, $v=3$. Therefore, surplus-value would be reduced but would not disappear: under the new conditions, $s = C' - (c+v) = 25 - (20+3) = 2$. The rate of surplus-value becomes $s/v = 2/3$, down from $3/3 = 1$.

Senior's self-serving conceptual error lies in the failure to distinguish between value created $(v+s)$ and value merely transferred (c). His analysis proceeds as if the labourer not only creates new value in the process of production but also recreates (rather than transfers) the value of the means of production. The consequence of this conceptual error is revealed by the absurdity of the conclusion. In actuality, "profit" would only disappear if surplus labour time were eliminated, that is, if the working day became no longer than necessary labour. In the present example, necessary labour is six hours.

CHAPTER X

The Working-Day

The creation of a normal working-day is, therefore, the product of a protracted civil war, more or less dissembled, between the capitalist class and the working class. (p. 283)

We have recently determined that surplus-value arises because of the discrepancy between the value and use-value of the commodity labour-power. This discrepancy manifests itself, in terms of time, as the difference between necessary labour time (corresponding to the value of labour-power) and the length of the working day (during which labour-power is used as labour and creates value). The difference between the length of the working day and necessary labour time is surplus labour time. Surplus-value is created during surplus labour time. Thus the determination of the length of the working day acquires paramount importance at this point in the exposition.

The working day, then, is the sum of two parts: necessary and surplus labour time. While necessary labour time can be said to be established for any particular period, surplus labour time is not strictly fixed, though it is bounded below and above. The working day must, on the one hand, be greater than necessary labour time and, on the other hand, be less than 24 hours. The upper limit has both a physiological and a social basis.

In the purchase and sale of any commodity, the buyer obtains its use-value while the seller receives the exchange-value of the commodity expressed in money. This is as true of labour-power as of any commodity and it is the exchange of equivalents which provides the basis for a struggle between employers and workers over the length of the working day. The capitalist, in effect, argues that as a purchaser he has a right to the full use-value of the commodity he has bought. The worker responds that an extension of the working day to the point that the reproduction of his labour-power is impaired means that he is not receiving the full value for his commodity. This clash of rights is resolved through class struggle, the outcome of which is decided by force. Along with Marx, we shall trace the specific forms this struggle took in England during the 19th century, but first we shall outline the forces which led to the development of the capitalist's desire for surplus labour time.

The exploitative extraction of surplus labour — the appropriation of a portion of the productive activity of one class by another class — did not originate with capitalism. In feudal societies, for example, peasants owe a portion of their labour time to the feudal lord. Here, in the institution of the corvée, the extraction of surplus labour appears in undisguised form. Marx refers to the various forms of surplus labour within different modes of production at several points in *Capital*.

As we pointed out in a previous chapter, M-C-M, the formula for capital in the sphere of circulation, has no inherent limit, in contrast to C-M-C, which is limited by a specific set of wants. Now, it is precisely the implication of this difference for production that determines a mode of production's desire for surplus labour. As soon as a society becomes dominated by production for exchange-value as opposed to production for use, the desire for surplus labour breaks through natural limits or wants. Thus, the Boyard of Wallachia who produces commodities for foreign markets exhibits the same hunger for surplus labour time as the English capitalist investing in a cotton factory. Both Boyard and capitalist seek to extend surplus labour time either through an increase in the corvée, in the case of the Boyard, or the extension of the working day, in the case of the capitalist. Since, as we observed earlier, capitalism is generalized commodity production, it is the capitalist mode of production which has a demand for the extension of labour time as a structural characteristic of the functioning of the economic system.

In those branches of production where the English Factory Acts (which were legislative attempts to limit the working day) had no application, such as lace-making, potteries, match-making, etc., Marx demonstrates that capital squandered human life at a frightening rate. This profligacy is not ultimately determined by the morality, ill will, or intent of individual capitalists, but rather is the result of a social process brought about through the interplay of objective economic conditions that ensure that personified capital (individuals in their role as capitalists) becomes avaricious or ceases to exist. Competition and accumulation are the mechanisms which determine the "common morality" of capitalists.

Capitalism introduced revolutionary new social relations and these relations in turn led to a revolution in the mode of production. The historical development specific to capitalism, the transition from manufacture to modern industry, was to have a powerful effect on the length of the working day. In part this was a function of the expanded weight of constant, as opposed to variable, capital in the productive process. This dramatic increase in constant capital produced a need for rapid turnover that led, among other things, to specific forms of work scheduling that permit continual and constant use of the means of production. The relay or shift-work system is one among a number of devices that capital introduced in order to increase the production of surplus-value.

The continual push of capital in the direction of the extension of the working day seems to be counter-productive in the final analysis. The continual extension of the working day in the interests of the development of absolute surplus-value would seem to be limited by the fact that the premature death and exhaustion of the workers would preclude the reproduction of the working class. However, historical experience has demonstrated that there is a constant excess of population relative to the needs of the expansion of capital (a subject to which Marx returns later in Volume I) and this excess permits capital to ignore the full force of the constraint that labour-power be able to reproduce itself. Indeed, no individual capitalist can afford to take these considerations into account, because free competition imposes the inherent laws of capitalist production in the shape of coercive laws governing the behaviour of individual producers. Thus, in the struggle over the working day, the working class must ultimately rely on its own strength and not on the collective rationality of the capitalist class.

The establishment of the normal working day was the result of a long and arduous class struggle. In the area of legislation, the struggle has been reflected in two different types of laws, corresponding to two distinct historical periods. Initially, as capitalism was developing, the capitalist class exerted pressure on the state to legislate a longer working day. Previous legislation, a product of the feudal period, embodied values, habits and economic relations of the prior mode of production.

After centuries of encroachment on traditional rights and norms, the last quarter of the 18th century witnessed a seemingly boundless extension of the working day. It was this trend which initiated a reaction by the working class, a reaction which took the form of a movement for legislative change. One consequence was the enactment in 1833 of a Factory Act which defined a normal working day of 12 hours for children and adolescents. By 1838, the working class had taken up the Ten Hours Bill as a central demand, an economic corollary to the Six Points of the Chartist Movement. The Chartists were a working-class political movement that struggled for the democratization of English political life. The implementation of the Six Points of the People's Charter (seeking electoral reforms such as an end to property qualifications for voting) was seen as an important step in a general restructuring of English society.

The balance of class forces in the 1840's favoured the passage of a Ten Hours Bill, for the ruling bloc was split over the question of free trade, i.e., the repeal of the Corn Laws (which imposed restrictions on the importation of grain). The split between landlord and industrial capitalist was reflected in the positions of political parties, the Tory Party representing the interests of the former and the Liberals those of the latter. Consequently, the political leadership of the industrialists attempted to enlist the support of the working class by adopting the Ten Hours Act as part of its program. The immediate result was the relatively modest Factory Act of 1844, which extended coverage of the 1833 Act to women over 18 and attempted to remedy abuses in the relay system. The practical effect of the Bill was a general 12-hour day, since any legislation affecting the employment of women and children was de facto extended to men in a heterogeneous work force.

The period of 1846-1847 was one of intense class struggle. On the one hand, the struggle within the ruling bloc resulted in the repeal of the Corn Laws. On the other hand, the Tory Party passed the Ten Hours Act of 1848 in response to the extra-parliamentary pressure of the Ten Hours Act Movement and as a means of revenge upon the industrialists. This Act effectively reduced the working day to 10 hours duration. In the face of the reduction of surplus-value, capital waged an extra-parliamentary petition campaign, lowered wages, initiated layoffs, etc. The campaign was largely unsuccessful until a change in the relationship of class forces gave it new impetus.

The political defeat of the Chartist Movement in England and of revolutionary movements generally throughout Europe in 1848 lessened the political impact of the proletariat and contributed to the unification of the ruling bloc in the face of the common working-class threat. The new campaign consisted of firings of youth and women, restoration of night work, refusal of time for nourishment, and various other tactics permitted by loopholes in the 10 hours legislation. The lower court system, which was staffed by the manufacturers and their associates, refused to uphold charges under the Act of 1848. The campaign culminated in a higher court decision which declared that the Act of 1848 was null and void. This decision sparked a new and furious response from the working class, which saw 40 years of agitation and effort coming to nought. The workers' response was so forceful and direct that a Factory Act of 1850 was quickly enacted and this act was henceforth extended to new industries and areas.

Marx felt that *Capital* could play a useful role in the working-class struggle to extend factory legislation. He mentions in the Preface to the first German edition of Volume I that one of the main functions of the numerous concrete examples incorporated in the text is to provide a model for working-class political action.

CHAPTER XI

Rate and Mass of Surplus-Value

With a given rate of surplus-value, and a given value of labour-power, therefore, the masses of surplus-value produced vary directly as the amounts of variable capitals advanced. (p. 290)

In the chapter on the rate and mass of surplus-value, Marx begins with a simple point, but draws from this point a number of profound consequences. An assumption (soon to be relaxed) which underlies the chapter is that necessary labour time is fixed.

As we have seen, given a particular duration of necessary labour, a working day of specific length yields a rate of surplus-value which is the ratio of surplus to necessary labour time. During necessary labour time, the worker reproduces value equal to that of his subsistence; this value comprises the variable capital paid to the worker in the form of wages. During surplus labour time, the worker produces surplus-value for the capitalist. The amount of surplus-value produced by an individual worker may then be expressed as the product of the variable capital paid as his wage and the rate of surplus-value; that is $s=v(s/v)=v(a'/a)$, where s is the surplus-value produced, v the variable capital employed, a' the duration of surplus labour, and a that of necessary labour.

Now, a capitalist employs not one but many workers and realizes the surplus-value produced by each. Therefore, the total amount or mass of surplus-value realized by the capitalist (S) is the product of the number of workers employed, n, and the surplus-value produced by an individual worker. Thus, $S=ns=n(v \cdot s/v)=V(s/v)=V(a'/a)$. Here, $V=nv$ is the total amount of variable capital advanced by the capitalist for his workers' wages. (Note that Marx, at one point, uses the symbol $P=v$ to represent the value of an average labour-power.)

Therefore, the mass of surplus-value realized by the

capitalist depends not only on the rate of surplus-value, that is, the degree of exploitation of labour-power, but also upon the amount of variable capital advanced by the capitalist. Under the assumption of a fixed value of labour-power, the amount of variable capital is directly proportional to the number of workers employed. A decrease in the rate of surplus-value can be compensated by an increase in variable capital and, within limits, a decrease in variable capital can be compensated by a lengthening of the working day.

We have seen that a capitalist divides his capital into constant and variable components, the former component advanced for means of production and the latter for labour-power. Since the value of constant capital is merely transferred to the product, it takes no part in the production of new value and hence of surplus-value. In the present chapter, we have discovered that the mass of surplus-value is dependent upon the magnitude of variable capital (and independent of the magnitude of constant capital). Thus, a capitalist operating in a sphere of production employing relatively little constant capital would appear to be at a competitive advantage since he produces more surplus-value in proportion to total capital advanced. That is, he would realize a relatively high rate of profit. Marx deals with the division of capital into its constant and variable components later in Volume I, most prominently in Chapter XXV. For the present, however, he notes that the law that the amount of surplus-value is dependent upon the relative division of a capital into its constant and variable parts seems to contradict appearances: capitalists in spheres of production with relatively large variable capital components do not generally realize greater than average rates of profit. This apparent contradiction is resolved in Volume III, where Marx takes up the question of the transformation of values into prices and the determination of rates of profit in different spheres of production. For the present, however, Marx resists the temptation to proceed directly to the level of appearances, a temptation to which vulgar economy succumbs. The goal of *Capital,* indeed the goal of scientific enterprise in general, is the explanation of appearances. However, to seek explanation at the level of phenomenal reality is generally self-defeating. As a scientific theorist, Marx instead seeks to probe beneath appearances, to uncover the processes which ultimately account for the phenomena appearing at the surface of society.

Assuming a fixed value of labour-power and a prevailing rate of surplus-value, each worker employed produces a specific quantity of surplus-value. In order for a capitalist to support himself on this surplus-value and have surplus-value left over to reinvest so as to increase the scale of production, he must necessarily employ some minimum number of workers. Moreover, the capital at the disposal of the capitalist must be sufficient, not only to pay these workers' wages (from its variable component), but also to supply them with requisite means of production (from its constant component). Therefore, the minimum amount of capital which a capitalist must have at his disposal is partly a function of the ratio of constant to variable capital in a given sphere of production.

Suppose, for example, that the rate of surplus-value is 100% and that a worker's weekly wage (an expression of the value of his labour-power) is $100. Each worker, then, produces $100 surplus-value in a week's labour. Suppose, further, that a capitalist consumes at twice the rate of a labourer, i.e., $200 per week, and requires an additional $100 per week to increase the scale of production. Under these circumstances, the capitalist initially would need to supply a weekly variable capital of $300 to pay the three workers necessary to produce $300 of surplus-value. The total capital investment, however, is dependent upon the value of constant capital set in motion by three workers, a value which will vary from one sphere of production to another. If this value is relatively large, the minimal capital required for production will also be relatively large.

Originally, capitalism transforms the social relations of production by subordinating labour to capital. However, the mode of production is unchanged. In the forthcoming chapters, Marx traces how capitalism transforms the mode of production itself.

PART IV

Production of Relative Surplus-Value

CHAPTER XII

The Concept of Relative Surplus-Value

But when surplus-value has to be produced by the conversion of necessary labour into surplus-labour, it by no means suffices for capital to take over the labour-process in the form under which it has been historically handed down, and then simply to prolong the duration of that process. The technical and social conditions of the process, and consequently the very mode of production must be revolutionized before the productiveness of labour can be increased. (pp. 298-299)

In Chapter X, Marx analyzed the working day into its two components: necessary labour time, during which the worker reproduces the value of his subsistence; and surplus labour time during which surplus-value is produced for the capitalist. The value of the worker's subsistence is the value of his labour-power, incorporated in his wage. Up to this point in the text, the value of labour-power has been assumed to be a fixed quantity.

The rate of surplus-value is simply the ratio between the two portions of the working day, between surplus and necessary labour time. If necessary labour time is fixed, the rate of surplus-value can only be altered through change in the length of the working day and with it, change in surplus labour time.

However, if the value of labour-power decreases, necessary labour time is of a consequence curtailed, and the rate of surplus-value will increase without an increase in the length of the workday.

Since the value of labour-power reflects the value of the commodities comprising the worker's subsistence, the value of labour-power is decreased by cheapening these commodities. This cheapening can be effected directly, by increasing productivity in those sectors of the economy which produce subsistence goods, or indirectly, by productivity gains in sectors supplying means of production (raw materials and instruments of labour) to subsistence goods industries. Productivity gains in the production of a particular commodity, then, only affect the value of labour-power if (and to the extent that) the commodity contributes directly or indirectly to workers' subsistence.

Marx terms increases in the rate of surplus-value which reflect the cheapening of the value of labour-power (and, thus, a shortening of necessary labour time), "relative surplus-value." Increases in the rate of surplus-value which are a result of the lengthening of the working day are termed "absolute surplus-value."

Now, individual capitalists in subsistence goods industries are not directly motivated to increase productivity so as to decrease the value of labour-power. Rather, the motivation is indirect and functions through the agency of competition. A more extensive analysis of competition appears later in *Capital,* although Marx offers a brief discussion of this mechanism here. As usual, a crucial distinction is drawn between the inner workings of the economy and the manner in which these factors are manifested on the surface of society and in the minds of individuals.

A capitalist who realizes an increase in productivity through some social or technical change in the mode of production, that is, one who is able to produce more use-values of a particular variety with a given quantity of labour, experiences a competitive advantage. Since the social value of a commodity depends upon socially necessary labour time and not upon labour time for an extraordinarily efficient producer, an efficient producer is able to dispose of his products at a price above what may be thought of as their "individual" value. Even if an efficient producer must sell his commodities below their social value, as a consequence of raising supply above demand, so long as price exceeds individual value, productivity gains result in increased surplus-value. Since an efficient producer need not increase his workers' wages; the workers, in effect, reproduce the value of their labour-power in less time, and the capitalist realizes a special sort of relative surplus-value. This sort of relative surplus-value is temporary as well as special; for as soon as the new method of production and, with it, productivity gains, become general in an industry, the social value of the product falls to its individual value.

Therefore, capitalists in all sectors are motivated to increase productivity by revolutionizing the mode of production so as to gain (temporary) competitive advantage. To the extent that this process affects sectors of the economy involved in the production of workers' subsistence goods, the value of labour-power is permanently cheapened, and relative surplus-value is realized by capitalists generally.

CHAPTER XIII

Cooperation

The combined working-day produces, relatively to an equal sum of isolated working-days, a greater quantity of use-values, and, consequently, diminishes the labour-time necessary for the production of a given useful effect. (p. 311)

We have seen how relative surplus-value arises from increases in productivity, either temporarily, for an individual capitalist when he realizes an advantage over his competitors, or permanently, for the capitalist class as a whole when the means of subsistence are cheapened. Increases in productivity imply changes in the mode of production, whether these changes are of a social or a technical nature. Since social changes in production antedated technical ones in the historical development of capitalism, Marx begins his examination of increased productivity under capitalism with a discussion of simple forms of cooperation. The next chapter extends his discussion to division of labour and manufacture. Finally, in the chapter on machinery and modern industry, which concludes the section on relative surplus-value, Marx demonstrates how capitalism revolutionizes the technical basis of production.

By cooperation, Marx means the simultaneous employment of a number of workers in unified productive activity, whether or not this employment entails a division of labour. Indeed, in the present chapter, the sort of cooperation considered is simple or elementary, employing at most, rudimentary differentiation of tasks.

Nonetheless, even elementary forms of cooperation result in productivity gains. As Marx puts it, the combined or social working day of the collective labourer produces a greater quantity of use-values than the separate workdays of individual labourers. He outlines a number of processes through which these productivity gains are realized. To summarize briefly: (1) When a large number of workers are employed simultaneously, individual differences in efficiency tend to cancel each other out. Therefore, a capitalist employing many workers employs, on average, average social labour. (2) When production is undertaken on a large scale, economies in the employment of certain elements of constant capital (e.g., buildings) are realized. These economies produce not only relative surplus-value, by cheapening commodities, but also an increased rate of profit. This last effect is considered at length in Volume III of *Capital*. (3) When a number of labourers coordinate their activity, they are able to undertake collective tasks which they are unable to perform individually. (4) Further, social contact among workers spurs them on to greater individual effort. (Interestingly, recent research in social psychology, with human beings and other species of animals, confirms Marx's observation.) (5) Certain kinds of tasks are more efficiently performed collectively, even in the absence of division of labour. (6) The availability of large numbers of workers facilitates their strategic employment in tasks (e.g., harvesting) which require that work be carried out at particular points in time. (7) Finally, the simultaneous employment of a large number of workers permits the extension or contraction of the "field of labour," the physical arena in which work takes place, as required by the particular task.

If a number of labourers are to work cooperatively, it is necessary that their work be organized, coordinated and supervised. This coordinating function is common to all modes of production in which work is undertaken collectively; it is not unique to capitalism. On the other hand, supervision under capitalism has another, non-universal, aspect. Because of the opposition of interests between workers and capitalists, the capitalist must keep workers under constant surveillance. As capitalism develops, these twin functions of supervision and surveillance increasingly fall to specialized workers, for example, managers and foremen.

In capitalism, associated labour takes place only under the aegis of the capitalist. Indeed, labourers work collectively only because their individual labour-powers have been purchased by a particular capitalist and set in motion under his direction. It therefore appears as if the increased productivity of collective labour is a product of capital itself. This appearance is reinforced by the historical development from individual commodity production, based on individual ownership of the means of production, to capitalism.

CHAPTER XIV

Division of Labour and Manufacture

It towered up as an economic work of art, on the broad foundation of the town handicrafts, and of the rural domestic industries. At a given stage in its development, the narrow technical basis on which manufacture rested, came into conflict with requirements of production that were created by manufacture itself. (p. 347)

SECTION 1. TWO-FOLD ORIGIN OF MANUFACTURE

Manufacture is a mode of production based upon a division of handicraft labour in the workplace. Historically, manufacture arises from its handicraft basis as a result of two opposite processes. The first process is one of combining formerly independent handicrafts under the control of a single capitalist. Artisans who previously functioned as independent commodity producers now pursue their crafts cooperatively, each responsible for a particular phase in the production of a commodity. A true division of labour arises as soon as these separate handicrafts lose their independent character and become specialized to the particular functions (detailed processes) required in the manufacture of a commodity.

Alternatively, manufacture can develop from the division of a previously unitary handicraft into component detail processes. Formerly independent artisans, each of whom undertakes all of the various stages in the fabrication of a product, are collected under the control of a capitalist. At first, their mode of working is unchanged: though they labour cooperatively for the capitalist, each still produces the whole, rather than a partial, product. However, for reasons of efficiency, a division of labour among the workers is eventually instituted and what was formerly a unitary process of production undertaken by many labourers working in parallel comes to be divided into a sequence of detail processes, each accomplished by specialists.

An essential aspect of manufacture, elaborated later in the chapter, is its continued basis in the handicraft or handicrafts from which it arose. True, manufacture rationalizes handicraft production through the institution and development of a division of labour. Yet, handicraft skill remains the foundation on which manufacture rests and, therefore, human beings are the fundamental components comprising its productive mechanism.

SECTION 2. THE DETAIL LABOURER AND HIS IMPLEMENTS

The development of a division of labour in manufacture results in increases in productivity. These productivity gains have several sources. First, workers who specialize in a particular detail process become expert in that process. Secondly, the division of work into a number of detail processes facilitates the development and perfection of each. Improved working methods developed by specialists in a particular process are communicated to their fellows and to new workers who are trained in the specialty. Thirdly, the working day of the detail labourer is employed more efficiently than that of an artisan who performs serially the several phases in the fabrication of a product. For the work of the artisan is constantly interrupted as he directs and redirects his activity from one partial process to another.

Just as the division of labour in manufacture perfects the activity of the worker, so too it improves the tools that the worker employs. Tools become specialized to particular tasks and, as a consequence, the productive process as a whole is made more efficient.

SECTION 3. THE TWO FUNDAMENTAL FORMS OF MANUFACTURE: HETEROGENEOUS MANUFACTURE, SERIAL MANUFACTURE

Marx begins this section by differentiating what he terms the two fundamental forms of manufacture. In heterogeneous manufacture, the various parts of a completed article are fabricated separately and are united in the finished product only in a final assembly operation. The manufacture of watches serves as an example of heterogeneous manufacture. It is largely incidental which partial products are fabricated under the control of the capitalist by workers labouring for him and which are obtained as commodities to furnish raw materials for the productive process.

In serial manufacture, the second form of manufacture, articles produced or parts of these articles pass from one to another of a sequence of detail processes. One worker (or set of workers) in this sequence receives the subject of his labour directly from another and, in turn, passes on the partial product to a third. The fabrication of needles provides an example of serial manufacture.

In manufacture, in contrast to production by independent artisans, all aspects of the production of an article occur simultaneously, each undertaken by a specialist. The simultaneity of the various aspects of the productive process is a consequence of the cooperative nature of manufacture. However, as has been seen, the particular form of cooperation in manufacture, the division of labour in the workplace, is created by the manufacturing system from its handicraft foundation.

The interrelated nature of the division of labour enforces standards of uniformity on labour within the workplace. Previously, these standards were manifested only externally through the workings of the law of value. That is, an independent producer of commodities is constrained to spend no more labour time in production than is socially necessary so as to realize the value of his labour when he exchanges his commodity product. The mechanism is indirect, working through competition and the market. However, in manufacture, a worker who takes more time than average to complete a detail process creates a bottleneck in the productive process itself.

The smooth operation of the process of production in manufacture requires not only that workers labour uniformly but also that the division of labour into its various detail processes be quantitatively correct. That is, detail operations which are accomplished relatively quickly require proportionately fewer workers than operations which are relatively time-consuming. Because workers are available only in integral quantities (a capitalist cannot employ part of a worker), the proportional division of labour among the detail processes comprising the manufacture of an article implies that there exists a certain minimum number of workers that can be employed efficiently in a particular industry. Likewise, the expansion of production requires that, apart from savings in labour (e.g., of supervision) produced by increases in scale, employment must be expanded by multiples of the minimal productive unit.

We have seen how manufacture can arise through the combination of formerly independent handicrafts. Marx explains that the further development of manufacture sometimes witnesses the amalgamation of previously independent factories. Therefore, a manufacturer may acquire what was previously an independent supplier of raw materials, converting these raw materials from externally procured commodities to partial products in a single process of production. Marx indicates, however, that this sort of "vertical integration" is typical of the later period of modern machine industry. The integration of several manufacturers is limited by the essential handicraft character of manufacture.

Although machinery is developed and employed to a limited extent in the manufacturing period, manufacture continues to find its basis in handicraft labour; however, the social nature of work is transformed by the division of labour. Workers literally become the parts of the human mechanism employed in manufacture. The specialization of work is partially based upon, and partially develops, individual differences among workers. In particular, differences in skill and training arise and there develops a consequent differentiation in the value of labour-power. Though the factory system develops a general differentiation of skilled and unskilled labour, it also produces a general cheapening in the value of labour-power, for even relatively skilled factory workers require less skill and training than independent handicrafters.

SECTION 4. DIVISION OF LABOUR IN MANUFACTURE, AND DIVISION OF LABOUR IN SOCIETY

The production and exchange of commodities presupposes a social division of labour. In the present section, Marx explores the development of the social division of labour and its relation to the division of labour within the workplace characteristic of manufacture.

Just as the division of labour in manufacture has a twofold origin, so the division of labour in society originates in two opposed processes. In all societies, there exists at least a rudimentary division of labour based upon, for example, sex and age differences. The division of labour in society develops partially as an elaboration of this rudimentary basis. Alternatively, it may be observed that different primitive societies produce different goods. As these societies are brought into relation with one another through the exchange of their products as commodities, a larger and more differentiated society is created.

The division of labour in society and that in manufacture are mutually related. On the one hand, capitalism requires the development of commodity production, which, in turn, presupposes social differentiation as a motivation for exchange. On the other hand, the system of manufacture further develops and elaborates the social division of labour. In particular, the development of manufacture in one industry spurs its development in other related industries, for example, in suppliers of raw materials.

Though there are several similarities between the division of labour in manufacture and that in society generally, and though the two are related in the manner outlined above, there is this fundamental difference: the division of labour in society is based upon the production of different commodities by independent, i.e., separate, producers; in contrast, within a single factory, partial products are not different commodities owned by the workers who produce them. Rather, the only commodity produced is the final product of the internal division of labour, and this product is the property of the capitalist under whose aegis production takes place. In a capitalist society, consequently, the social division of labour is regulated only indirectly, by mechanisms of the market and of competition, while the division of labour in the factory is controlled directly by the capitalist. The orderliness of the internal division of labour is counterposed to the anarchic nature of the division of labour in society. Marx mentions that there are other forms of society which directly regulate the social division of labour.

Capitalist production and, hence, the manufacturing system, require first that the capitalist possesses the capital to purchase means of production and labour-power. Additionally, however, the labourer must be separated from the means of production so that he is compelled to sell his labour-power as a commodity. Commodity production exists in different types of social systems, and the social division of labour is more general still; yet, the division of labour in the workplace which characterizes manufacture is specific to capitalism in that it requires the separation of the labourer from his means of production.

SECTION 5. THE CAPITALISTIC CHARACTER OF MANUFACTURE

We have seen how the division of labour in manufacture implies a minimum number of labourers for efficient production. As this division of labour develops and grows more complex, the smallest number of workers who must be employed grows as a consequence. The capitalist must, therefore, have an increasing amount of variable capital at his disposal in order to undertake production. In addition, since workers have to be provided with means of production, the constant portion of capital grows alongside the variable portion. Indeed, because the development of the division of labour is associated with increases in productivity, constant capital increases more quickly than variable (unless, of course, there are off-setting productivity gains in the industries supplying means of production).

As in the case of simple cooperation, discussed in the previous chapter, increased productivity due to the division of labour in the workplace appears to be a function of capital, since this division of labour is created and directed by the capitalist. Unlike simple cooperation, which does not radically alter the nature of the individual's labour, manufacture creates the detail labourer, who is capable of functioning only as a part of the larger human productive mechanism. Manufacture, therefore, furthers the separation of intellectual and physical labour, a separation which begins in simple cooperation and, as is demonstrated in the next chapter, develops still further in the period of modern machine industry. On the one hand, then, manufacture results in productivity gains which serve as a source of relative surplus-value for the capitalist. On the other hand, these gains in productivity are achieved at the expense of the worker, by limiting and confining his labour to a narrow sphere.

Although manufacture is, as we have seen, a powerful force in the development of capitalism, it is essentially limited by its technical basis in handicrafts. Marx continually emphasizes this point in the course of the present chapter. The mechanism of manufacture has human beings as its parts and, as a result, these workers have some degree of power which they can exercise against the capitalist. However, one of the ultimate products of the manufacturing period is machinery. Machinery eventually revolutionizes the technical basis of production and, therefore, removes the constraints on capital which are present in the manufacturing period.

CHAPTER XV

Machinery and Modern Industry

Modern Industry never looks upon and treats the existing form of a process as final. The technical basis of that industry is therefore revolutionary, while all earlier modes of production were essentially conservative. (p. 457)

Modern industry revolutionized the technical basis of production through the conversion of the instruments of labour from tools to machines. The same forces for innovation that ensured the development of the social productivity of labour in manufacture continued to operate to bring about the transition to machine production. By continually revolutionizing the forces of production, modern industry completes the development of the capitalist mode of production begun by manufacture. The development of the productive forces through the use of machinery is the historical task of the capitalist mode of production.

A useful way of approaching this chapter is to organize the various sections around the theme of change. The section headings specify change at various levels and establish interrelationships among these levels. Thus, the first section describes the technical change in the means of production that results from the development of the new mode of production. Section 2 delineates the impact of the new technology and means of production on value relations, specifically on exchange-value and the division of capital into its constant and variable components. Marx proceeds to examine the relationship between change in value relations and technology, on the one hand, and in the social relations of production, on the other. Thus, Sections 3 through 7 deal with the impact on the working class of change at the level of value and technology. Section 8 details the effects of the new mode of production on older forms of social production such as handicraft and domestic industry; Section 10 does the same for the sphere of agricultural production. Section 9 shows how the development of the forces and relations of production is reflected at the political level, as the capitalist market becomes unable to ensure the reproduction of labour-power. While change originates at the level of value and technology, it is clear that the relation between levels is reciprocal, with changes at the social and political level exercising a reactive effect on value and technology.

The development of the system of manufacture rested on change in the social organization of the labour process, while the development of modern industry is given its impetus by change in the material means of production. Thus, Marx begins the chapter on modern industry by differentiating between machines and tools. Machinery consists of three parts: the motor mechanism, the transmitting mechanism, and the working machine. The working machine is a mechanism that performs the operations which were formerly undertaken by the detail labourer. Consequently, the labour process is freed from the immediate constraints imposed by the human body.

In the course of the development of modern industry, an important turning point is reached in the transition from simple cooperation among machines to a complex system of machinery. Simple cooperation of machines corresponds to simple cooperation generally in that there is no complex mechanical division of labour. In contrast, a system of machinery reproduces the division of labour of manufacture freed from the subjective limitations of man.

The transition from manufacture to modern industry is brought about by the internal development of the system of manufacture through the evolution of the machine. Put another way, the machine is the material agency of the demise of the manufacturing system. However, at first, the production of machinery can only proceed on a handicraft basis. The handicraft production of machinery imposes serious limitations on the development of modern industry and provides the impulse for the production of machinery by machinery, completing the work of the industrial revolution.

The transition to machine production, a transition which takes place at the level of the technical means of production, has an important impact on value relations. Marx begins the second section of the chapter by asking how it is that tremendously expensive machinery is able to reduce the value of commodities in comparison to production by relatively inexpensive tools in manufacture. Answering this question, Marx points out that a machine only transfers its value to the product piecemeal over its whole life in the productive process. A machine generally has a longer life than a tool and therefore will have less average wear and tear in the process of production. However, the crucial determinant of reduction in value of the product is the increased productiveness of the machine. While the value a machine transmits to products per day remains greater than that of a tool, the number of commodities it produces per day is much greater. Consequently, the value transferred to each individual product declines. There is a general reduction in the value of commodities with the development of modern industry.

While the value of commodities is reduced, the proportion of constant capital increases at the expense of variable capital. Marx takes up the topic of changes in the division of capital between its constant and variable components later in Volume I and elsewhere in *Capital*. If commodities are to be cheapened, employment of machinery is necessarily limited by the amount of labour time that it replaces, a quantity which must be greater than the amount of labour that it takes to produce the machine. For the capitalist, who is interested only in the augmentation of the surplus-value that he appropriates, the use of machinery is further limited by the fact that only part of the labour employed in production is paid (i.e., necessary labour). Therefore, for a capitalist to be motivated to adopt it, a machine must cost less than the labour-power that it replaces. For example, imagine that a machine saves ten hours of labour and costs the equivalent of six hours of labour; suppose further that the rate of surplus-value is 100%, so a 10-hour working day costs the capitalist the equivalent of five hours' labour. Even though under these circumstances the machine would produce commodities more cheaply, it is not in the interest of the capitalist to introduce it since it would cost him more than the labour-power that it replaces.

Changes at the level of value and technology produce important changes in the structure and behaviour of the working class. First, the employment of women and children becomes possible on a greatly expanded scale. While this development could provide the basis for a new pattern of relations between the sexes and between parents and children, more immediately it depreciates the value of labour-power. For the same or slightly higher wages, a capitalist is able to obtain much more labour. The employment of women and children under the most wretched conditions leads to poor health and high mortality rates among the working class. Secondly, the vast increase in constant capital which accompanies the introduction of machinery is an enormous stimulant to the extension of the working day. Capital's appetite for surplus labour now acquires new sources, such as the desire to recover investment before technological obsolescence overtakes constant capital. The need to bring constant capital in contact with living labour-power is heightened by the sheer size of invested capital. Through devices such as shift work (the relay system), capital attempts to reduce to a minimum the time during which the means of production are idle.

The use of machinery poses new problems for the capitalist. These problems disclose themselves whenever the innovative phase of production ends and productivity change is generalized throughout an industry. Now the surplus profits due to technological monopolies disappear and the result of revolutionizing the means of production is revealed to be an overall relative decrease in the use of labour-power. Since living labour-power is the ultimate source of surplus-value, the generation of surplus-value is curtailed. The eventual result is a fall in the rate of profit. The third impact of mechanization on the working class is the intensification of labour in the labour process. The immediate reaction of the capitalist to a falling rate of profit is to augment surplus labour time through an increase in absolute working time. Once the working-class movement has developed to a point where it is able to wage a struggle to limit the length of the working day, one of the mechanisms that remains available to the capitalist is the intensification of labour. This discussion reveals that labour time acquires a new dimension. Previously, duration was the sole measure of labour; now, intensity is taken into consideration as well. Intensification of labour, through the speed-up of machinery, acts as a powerful new source of surplus-value at a time when increases in absolute surplus-value are curtailed by the statutory limitation of the working day.

The new means of production are grouped in factories. These factories are places of employment in which the operation of production takes place independently of the worker. Human labour-power is homogenized as the old division of labour in the workplace is replaced by the division between operators and helpers. The specialization of the detail labourer, a product of the manufacturing system, is artificially reproduced in the factory system by riveting the worker to one machine. Thus the decline of interest in work combines with the complete separation of manual and intellectual labour to produce a new form of torment for the working class.

The identification of capitalism with the material means of production characteristic of modern industry causes the labouring class to revolt against this particular form of the means of production rather than against the social relations underlying them. Therefore, in the early period of development of the working class, the machine itself is perceived as the enemy of the class. The competition between the working man and the machine for employment develops the full force of this antagonism which is expressed, for example, in the Luddite movement.

The response of bourgeois political economy to the opposition of machine and worker within capitalism is to evolve explanations that attempt to justify or lessen the antagonism. In order to accomplish this purpose, economists developed the theory of compensation. According to this theory, the capital set free by mechanization represents means of subsistence which must be reunited with the worker in order to function as capital. Hence, industrialization represents only a temporary inconvenience to the worker. As Marx indicates, the theory of compensation is confused. The primary analytical error incorporated in the theory is the false identification of variable capital with workers' subsistence. True, variable capital is paid to workers in the form of wages, which are, in turn, spent for subsistence goods. But the subsistence goods themselves are not capital capable of employing workers. When a portion of capital formerly employed for wages is converted to constant capital, workers are let go. The fact that these workers' subsistence is consequently also "set free" does not provide variable capital for their employment. There is simply a decreased demand for subsistence goods. Industrialization can, indeed, increase the overall level of employment, though not through the mechanism of "compensation." Marx merely sketches this topic here; it is considered in detail in Chapter XXV.

As modern industry develops and the factory system is extended, the mode of production acquires an elasticity in its ability to reproduce itself. This elasticity is demonstrated in the industrial cycle of modern industry. Frantic periods of production are followed by crisis, stagnation and eventual recovery. Thus, the employment of the working class becomes more and more unstable and problematic. Since employment is a product of the interplay of accumulation and the increasing productivity of labour, greater and greater investments are required to maintain employment at a particular level. Investment is tied to the industrial cycle and to the cyclical movement of the rate of profit. Consequently, the working class finds itself alternately attracted and repelled by the factory system, depending upon the state of the business cycle.

Modern industry revolutionizes all other modes of production. Manufacture, handicrafts and domestic industry are completely transformed and eventually abolished in the rush of capitalist expansion. In constituting the factory system and periodically reconstituting a reduced sector of manufacture and domestic industry, the worst features of these earlier modes of production are accentuated. As soon as the limits to abuse of labour-power are encountered, the system of manufacture is ready to be replaced by modern industry. Thus, the Factory Acts artificially ripen the material elements necessary for the conversion of the manufacturing system and, in the process, hasten the decline of the small capitalist. While the Factory Acts advance the development of capitalism, they represent a conscious attempt to regulate the spontaneous actions of the economic system. As well as regulations pertaining to maximum hours of work, the Acts include regulations governing sanitation and education.

The spontaneous action of the capitalist mode of production

is to revolutionize continually the technical basis of industry. This revolution in the means of production results in a contradiction that is expressed as a difference between the demands of the technical division of labour for a worker who is adaptable and well-rounded and the social division of labour in its capitalist form which produces a worker whose knowledge and skills are fragmented and partial. The historical development of this antagonism creates the foundation upon which a socialist society can build as well as acting as a lever to promote the actual movement toward socialism.

The extension and augmentation of the Factory Acts stem from two sources. First, as exploitation is regulated in one direction, it rushes headfirst in another. Soon, abuses in the new area require the same legislative control as those in the earlier one. Secondly, the capitalists who must function under the regulations refuse to permit the continuation of competitive advantage to those not covered by legislation. The demand for equality of competition becomes a powerful force behind the extension of the Acts beyond their original purview.

The impact of modern industry is equally revolutionary in the sphere of agriculture. Old means of production and social forms corresponding to them are rendered obsolete, subsequently to be replaced by mechanized agriculture performed by wage labour. The class antagonism of the urban centres is thrust outward toward the rural periphery.

PART V

The Production of Absolute and of Relative Surplus-Value

CHAPTER XVI

Absolute and Relative Surplus-Value

The production of absolute surplus-value turns exclusively upon the length of the working-day; the production of relative surplus-value, revolutionizes out and out the technical processes of labour, and the composition of society. (p. 477)

In Part V, Marx draws together the discussion of absolute and relative surplus-value. The first chapter in this section situates capitalist production historically and explores the natural and social basis for the production of surplus-value.

The abstract consideration of the labour process which appeared earlier in Volume I led to a definition of productive labour as labour which produces use-values. From the point of view of capitalist production, and the division of labour in the workplace which it engenders, the definition of productive labour is both broadened and narrowed. Since, as a result of the division of labour in the workplace, particular commodities are no longer produced by individual workers but rather by collective labour, for an individual labourer to be productive it is no longer necessary for him to produce use-values directly but only to participate in their production. For example, a labourer such as a draftsman who engages in intellectual work necessary to commodity production, labours productively. However, capitalist production entails not only the production of commodities but also the production of surplus-value. For a worker to labour productively in the context of capitalism, therefore, it is necessary that he sell his labour-power to a capitalist and that he produce surplus-value for the capitalist. Marx takes up the question of productive and unproductive labour at greater length in Volume II of *Capital* and in *Theories of Surplus Value.*

We have seen how absolute surplus-value arises out of the prolongation of the working day beyond necessary labour time and, hence, requires merely the formal subjugation of labour to capital (that is, the sale of labour-power to, and its employment by, capital). We have also seen how relative surplus-value develops from the real subjugation of labour to capital, the revolutionizing of the social and technical aspects of the productive process itself. The real subjugation of labour to capital, then, develops upon a formal base.

At any given point in time, the rate of surplus-value is determined by the division of the working day into its components of necessary and surplus labour time. Consequently, the distinction between absolute and relative surplus-value appears arbitrary until we contemplate the ways in which surplus-value can be extended: either the working day can be lengthened or, alternatively, necessary labour can be contracted by increasing the productivity or intensity of labour.

The possibility of producing surplus-value has both a social and a natural basis. Necessary labour time is determined by the social productivity of labour and social standards of subsistence, on the one hand, and by natural wealth in means of subsistence and instruments of labour and naturally determined needs, on the other. However, the actual production of social surplus, the appropriation of this surplus by other than the direct producer, and the manner of that appropriation (e.g., by slavery, feudal rents, or wage labour) are historically dependent upon the development of specific social relations. Indeed, with the development of capitalism and the attendant rise in the social productivity of labour, natural limits on productivity decrease in importance.

Classical political economists such as Ricardo fail to place capitalism in its historical context. By treating the capitalist mode of production as natural and universal, they are unable to distinguish the nature and origin of surplus-value from the determination of its magnitude. Vulgar economy, for example in the person of Mill, further clouds the issue by failing to distinguish between the production of social surplus and the appropriation of this surplus. Thus, Mill treats as a capitalist the independent producer who works beyond necessary labour time and appropriates his own surplus product (whether for use or sale). Furthermore, the wage labourer working for a capitalist is seen as lending "capital" to his employer and sharing in the surplus that he produces.

CHAPTER XVII

Changes of Magnitude in the Price of Labour-Power and in Surplus-Value

---

The relative magnitudes of surplus-value and of price of labour-power are determined by three circumstances ... (p. 486)

Assuming that commodities exchange at their values and that the price of labour-power does not fall below its value, there are three factors which determine the relative magnitudes of the price of labour-power and of surplus-value. These factors are: the length of the working day; the intensity of labour; and the productivity of labour. Since the combined effect of simultaneous variation in two or three of these factors is determined in a straightforward manner from their separate effects, their separate effects are the primary subject of this chapter.

Assuming that the length of the working day and the intensity of labour remain unaltered, the amount of value created by a day's labour is fixed. The division of this value into the value of labour-power and surplus-value, however, is dependent upon the productivity of labour. Increased productivity (in industries producing consumption goods) cheapens labour-power and therefore extends surplus-value. Marx notes that, in this case, changes in surplus-value are indirect, brought about by variations in the value of labour-power. He goes on to point out that because of worker resistance to declining wages, increasing productivity can be followed by a smaller fall in the price of labour-power and a consequent smaller increase in surplus-value. Under these circumstances, labour-power exchanges above its value and, hence, workers share in productivity gains by commanding a wage which buys more use-values (i.e., their real wages rise). Yet it is important to realize that even as the workers' means of subsistence are extended, so long as the price of labour falls, surplus-value is augmented.

If the length of the working day and the productiveness of labour are held constant, the amount of value produced in a given time will be directly proportional to the intensity of labour, for labour more intense than the social average produces proportionately more value. The increment in value resulting from an increase in the intensity of labour would generally result in increases both in the price of labour-power and in surplus-value. The increase in the price of labour-power follows from the assumption that this commodity exchanges at (or at least, not below) its value and the observation that an increase in the intensity of labour produces more wear and tear of labour-power, which, in turn, must be compensated by greater wages. Since change in the intensity of labour produces changes in value created, the consequent variations in the value of labour-power and surplus-value result whether or not the change takes place in industries producing workers' subsistence goods. This effect, then, contrasts with that of changes in productivity, which produce (permanent) variations in the value of labour-power and surplus-value only when subsistence goods production is affected.

Assuming that the productiveness and intensity of labour do not change, the amount of value created in a working day varies in proportion to its length. A workday of increased length produces more surplus-value, by extending surplus labour time further beyond necessary labour time. The value of labour-power may increase as well, as a function of increased wear and tear of labour-power.

As we noted previously, simultaneous changes in the length of the working day, intensity of labor and productivity produce effects which are the cumulative product of variations in the individual factors. Marx analyzes two such cases which are of historical importance: decreasing productivity accompanied by an offsetting increase in the length of the workday; and increasing intensity and productivity of labour together with a partially offsetting contraction of the working day. In the latter case, Marx mentions that the greater quantities of use-values resulting from productivity gains and increased labour intensity provide the possibility of greater leisure for the workers. However, this possibility can never be realized to its full extent within capitalism inasmuch as labour time must extend beyond necessary labour. Were production to be organized socially, labour time could contract in this manner, although what would be considered necessary labour would expand to include a social fund for reserve and accumulation.

CHAPTER XVIII

Various Formulae for the Rate of Surplus-Value

> *Capital, therefore, is not only, as Adam Smith says, the command over labour. It is essentially the command over unpaid labour .... The secret of the self-expansion of capital resolves itself into having the disposal of a definite quantity of other people's unpaid labour. (p. 500)*

The rate of surplus-value may be variously expressed, for example, as the ratio of surplus-value to variable capital, of surplus-value to the value of labour-power (for which variable capital is exchanged), or of surplus labour (the creator of surplus-value) to necessary labour (the time during which the worker creates value equal to his wage). Now, it is also possible to express surplus-value as a proportion of value produced. Here, for example, we take the ratio of surplus labour to the length of the working day, of surplus-value (the product of surplus labour) to the value of the product (excluding value transferred from constant capital), or of surplus product (the use-value embodying surplus-value) to the total product (again, excluding the portion of the product corresponding to the value of transferred constant capital).

Although it is not incorrect to express surplus-value as a proportion of value created — after all, this formula follows from that for the rate of surplus-value — the practice can prove misleading for two reasons. First, since the ratio of the two portions of the working day (the rate of surplus-value) will always be larger than the proportion of the working day devoted to the production of surplus-value, the latter measure (if not clearly understood) can be taken to understate the degree of exploitation of labour. Secondly, and more seriously, the practice of dividing the working day into proportions of necessary and surplus labour creates the appearance that the worker and capitalist are in a partnership where each shares in the value of the product in proportion to his contribution to its production. According to this mistaken notion, the wage (the value equivalent of necessary labour) is conceived as the worker's share of value created, while surplus-value (corresponding to surplus labour) is viewed as the share accruing to the capitalist as a result of his investment.

So long as it is understood that the capitalist purchases the commodity labour-power and not labour (which is not a commodity), surplus labour may be termed "unpaid labour" and necessary labour, "paid labour." Surplus labour is unpaid in the sense that during this period, the worker creates value for which he receives no equivalent. In contrast, during necessary labour time, the labourer reproduces the value of his wage. It is by commanding the unpaid labour of workers that capital is able to expand its value.

PART VI

Wages

CHAPTER XIX

The Transformation of the Value (and Respectively the Price) of Labour-Power into Wages

---

On the surface of bourgeois society the wage of the labourer appears as the price of labour, a certain quantity of money that is paid for a certain quantity of labour. (p. 501)

The general mode of exposition and explanation in *Capital* is from the abstract to the concrete (or, better, from higher to lower levels of abstraction), from the inner mechanisms of society to their manifestation on the surface of society, from essence to appearance. On the surface of society, the labourer appears to sell his labour to the capitalist and, therefore, the labourer's wage appears to be the price of labour, the expression of the value of labour.

However, analysis shows the concepts of the value and price of labour to be irrational, fundamentally inconsistent with the labour theory of value. In general, the value of a commodity is determined by the socially necessary labour time for its production, and the price of a commodity is an expression of its value in money, albeit influenced by accidental disturbances due to supply and demand. (In fact, in Volume III of *Capital*, Marx introduces factors which lead to the systematic departure of price from value, but these factors need not be considered here.) How, then, is labour to be conceived as a commodity? Were labour considered a commodity, a given quantity of labour would express its own value, and if a worker were to be paid this value, the source of surplus-value would disappear. There would be no logical basis in the law of value (exchange of equivalents) for the worker to receive a wage of value less than that created by his labour. Furthermore, a commodity must exist in order to be sold. If a worker could embody his labour as a commodity, he could sell that commodity as an independent producer, realizing the full value of his labour, rather than labouring for a capitalist.

We conclude, then, that to retain the labour theory of value, we must conceive of the worker selling his labour-power, not labour. Labour, indeed, is not a commodity and, therefore, does not have value and cannot be exchanged. Labour, the use-value of labour-power, belongs to the capitalist once he purchases the commodity labour-power from the worker.

Though the underlying value relations entail the sale and purchase of the commodity labour-power, on the surface of society the transaction appears as the sale and purchase of labour. The appearance is irrational, as we have seen, but it is not unreal. However, to explain the appearance we must appeal to the underlying value relations. Classical political economy never successfully separates the underlying mechanisms from their appearance and, therefore, is led into inconsistency. Vulgar economy is concerned with the appearances only and fails to probe the fundamental sources of these appearances.

The wage form, that is, the appearance that the transaction between worker and capitalist entails the sale and purchase of labour, obscures the division of the working day into paid and unpaid components and, hence, obscures the source of surplus-value. Since the worker is, for example, paid an hourly wage determined by the value of labour-power and the length of the working day, it seems as if all his labour is paid, for there is no formal division of the workday into necessary and surplus labour. In the feudal corvée, the division between the peasant's labour for himself and for the lord is formal and clear. The slave, in contrast, appears to work only for his master and not at all for himself, though he must necessarily produce the value of his subsistence during a portion of his working day. The social relations of production in slavery, entailing the permanent ownership of the labour-power of the slave, make all labour appear to be unpaid. The social relations of production in capitalism, entailing the sale of labour-power by free labourers to capitalists, make all labour appear to be paid.

The appearance that the transaction between worker and capitalist involves the exchange of labour is reinforced by several phenomenal aspects of this transaction. The exchange appears similar to that of commodities in general. The use-value of labour-power is labour and, thus, to speak of the value or price of labour appears no more irrational than to speak of the value or price of commodities in general. Workers, in general, are paid only after supplying a given amount of labour. To the worker, then, changes in his wage appear as variations in the value of the labour that he supplies. The capitalist, on the other hand, conceives of labour as similar to the commodities he purchases for production: it is to his advantage to pay as little as possible for as much labour as possible. Finally, variations in wages over time (with changes in the length of the working day) and among workers (in relation to individual differences in productivity) reinforce the impression that labour is bought and sold as a commodity. However, in these cases, as in general, variations in wages can be traced to variations in the value of labour-power: in the first instance, change in the length of the working day alters the value of labour-power (e.g., through wear and tear) while, in the second, variation is produced by individual differences in the efficacy of labour-power.

CHAPTER XX

Time-Wages

The average price of labour is found, when the average daily value of the labour-power is divided by the average number of hours in the working-day. (p. 509)

Having accounted for the phenomenal form of wages in terms of the underlying mechanism determining the value of labour-power, Marx turns to a brief consideration of the two fundamental forms of wages: time-wages, treated in the present chapter; and piece-wages, discussed in the next.

We have seen that the value of labour-power resolves itself into the sum of values of the commodities which the worker must purchase to maintain himself and his family. This sum of values of the necessaries of life, then, becomes translated into the phenomenal form of the worker's nominal or money wage. The necessaries of life themselves comprise the worker's real wages.

Once the average daily price of labour-power and the average length of the working day are determined, the average hourly price of labour (the time-wage form) may be simply calculated as the quotient of these two quantities. Therefore, the price of labour is a function of the price of labour-power and the length of the working day. Daily or weekly wages are, in turn, products of the hourly price of labour and the length of the work-day and work week, respectively. Consequently, the price of labour may vary with or without producing variations in daily or weekly wages, and variations in daily or weekly wages may be unaccompanied by changes in the (hourly) price of labour.

The hourly price of labour is fixed as a social average. Therefore, a worker who is only partially employed, who works for less time than the social average, may fail to realize a socially average daily or weekly wage. A labourer who works a longer than average day realizes daily wages in excess of the social average. In fact, since the wear and tear on labour-power increases at a proportionately greater rate than the length of the working day, a worker who labours beyond the normal working day (the basis on which average wages are calculated) may receive overtime pay.

Since, for a fixed price of labour, the daily wage depends upon the length of the working day, when the price of labour is low a labourer must work a longer day to gain his subsistence. Alternatively, if the length of the working day is increased, without changing the daily wage, the price of labour declines. Under these circumstances, the mechanism of competition (analyzed incompletely here) ultimately causes a decline in nominal daily wages and in commodity prices. Since a longer day increases the supply of labour without affecting the supply of labour-power (the same number of workers supply more hours of work), competition among workers for employment results in a decline in the price of labour. Moreover, competition among capitalists produces an eventual decline in commodity prices. A more complete exposition of the mechanism of competition and its role in the determination of prices appears later in *Capital*.

CHAPTER XXI

Piece-Wages

> *Given piece-wage, it is naturally the personal interest of the labourer to strain his labour-power as intensely as possible . . . (p. 519)*

When a worker is paid time-wages, it appears as if he sells his labour to the capitalist. The analysis of the last chapter shows, however, that the value of labour-power underlies the time-wage form: time-wages are a converted form of the value (or price — the expression of value in money) of labour-power. Likewise, when a worker is paid piece-wages, it appears as if he sells the result of his labour to the capitalist. Once again, we are caught in an inconsistency unless we probe below the level of appearances.

A labourer working in a particular job will, on average, produce a certain number of products in a working day of fixed length. Dividing the daily value of labour-power by this average number of products yields a piece-rate. Clearly, by its mode of determination, the piece-rate results in a wage equal to the value of labour-power for a worker whose personal productivity is the social average. Individual differences in productivity are reflected in differences in wages.

Although piece-wages, then, are logically similar to time-wages, they have certain properties which are advantageous for the capitalist. Piece-wages provide a built-in mechanism for controlling the quality and intensity of labour, since the worker realizes a normal wage only if his work is of average quality and quantity. Because workers are paid in proportion to their output, they are motivated to increase the intensity of their labour and to acquiesce to lengthening of the working day. Though, in the short run, daily wages may rise, in the long run the price of labour depreciates. Piece-work also fosters an individualistic orientation among workers. Competition among workers yields differential rewards in relation to their personal productiveness, but it ultimately lowers the average wage and, hence, works to their collective detriment. For these and other reasons, Marx states that piece-wages are particularly well-suited to capitalist production.

When the length of the working day is fixed by law, as in the Factory Acts, piece-wages become an especially important means of increasing the rate of surplus-value. For with the length of the working day fixed, the amount of value produced can be increased only by heightening the intensity of labour. Piece-wages, we have seen, make it easier for the capitalist to raise the intensity of labour.

Since the piece-rate is determined by the average number of commodities produced in a working day, when productivity increases, the piece-rate must fall proportionately. However, the actual determination of the piece-rate is a source of struggle between workers and capitalists. And capitalists often use productivity changes as a pretext for decreasing the price of labour by increasing its intensity.

CHAPTER XXII

National Differences of Wages

> ***That which appears in these fluctuations of wages within a single country as a series of varying combinations, may appear in different countries as contemporaneous difference of national wages. (p. 524)***

By this point in the text, it is no doubt clear that the presentation in Volume I of *Capital* is nothing if not orderly. Yet, to us at least, the material on national differences in wages appeared to be a digression. It is our opinion that this material serves to illustrate the laws governing the determination of the value of labour-power (and, hence, wages) and the rate of surplus-value. In the previous discussion, these laws were employed to explain differences in wages over time. Contemporaneous international differences determined by the same laws are the subject of the present analysis. Marx says as much in the introductory paragraph of the chapter.

The same factors which determine the value of labour-power in a single nation must be taken into account in the analysis of international wage differences. Marx here enumerates a number of these factors, including: the value of the articles which comprise the worker's subsistence; the costs of apprenticeship and training; the prevalence of woman and child labour; the social productivity of labour; the length of the working day; and the intensity of labour.

In a particular nation, socially necessary labour time is figured at the average intensity of labour; the additional time taken for the production of a commodity by labour less intense than average is counted as wasted from the point of view of the creation of value. Internationally, the average intensity of labour varies from country to country. When products exchange on the international market, commodities produced in a nation with a relatively high intensity of labour have greater value (for a given time of production) than those produced in a nation where the intensity of labour is relatively low.

Though a more complex analysis of competition is postponed to Volume III, Marx previously explained that the mechanism of competition prevents productivity differences from determining permanent differences in value. To the degree that international competition is absent, international differences in productivity produce differences in value in the same manner as do variations in the intensity of labour.

More advanced countries, those in which the social productivity and intensity of labour are higher than average, produce a greater quantity of use-values of a particular variety in a given amount of labour time. Therefore, the amount of labour represented by a specific quantity of money is less in these countries than in less advanced countries. As Marx puts it, the value of money is less in the more advanced nations. Marx proceeds to argue that money-wages will consequently be higher in nations with more advanced capitalist modes of production, although differences in real wages depend upon variations in the price of subsistence goods.

The analysis of surplus-value revealed that the value of labour-power not only must be evaluated absolutely, but also must be compared with the amount of surplus-value produced. Consequently, even if real wages are higher in the more advanced nations, the rate of surplus-value may be higher as well.

PART VII

The Accumulation of Capital

Strictly speaking, the accumulation of capital involves an understanding of mechanisms that go beyond the framework of Volume I, inasmuch as the volume is a study of the capitalist production process. Capitalist accumulation involves circulation in addition to production as commodities exchange for one another, a process in which surplus-value is distributed among landowners, merchants and financiers as well as industrial capitalists. Thus, social production involves classes and fractions of capital outside the worker-capitalist relation. Landowners, merchants and financiers are all personifications of fractions of capital that play specific roles in social production. In this section of the text, Marx abstracts from the complications and complexities of the process of accumulation by assuming that the industrial capitalist sells at value and retains all of the surplus-value produced by the labourers under his employ. Abstraction allows Marx to reveal the inner mechanism of the process of accumulation, a mechanism which is only obscured by the intervention of circulation and by the division of surplus-value among landlord, merchant, industrialist and financier. The abstract understanding of accumulation achieved here in Volume I is complicated and extended later in *Capital*.

CHAPTER XXIII

Simple Reproduction

Capitalist production, therefore, under its aspect of a continuous connected process, of a process of reproduction, produces not only commodities, not only surplus-value, but it also produces and reproduces the capitalist relation; on the one side the capitalist, on the other the wage-labourer. (p. 542)

For society to continue to function, every process of production must of necessity be simultaneously a process of reproduction. As a society produces, it must make provision for the reproduction of means of production and labour-power that will be productively consumed in the future. In the present chapter, Marx examines "simple reproduction," a system of reproduction in which surplus-value is wholly expended as revenue by the capitalist for personal consumption. The capitalist class uses the surplus-product of society as its consumption fund. Since no surplus-value is spent to increase the scale of production, the capitalist continually reproduces the system at the same level. In a subsequent chapter, Marx investigates the case of expanded reproduction, where part of surplus-value is expended as new capital rather than as revenue. The capitalization of surplus-value is termed accumulation.

Viewing capitalism as a system of reproduction deepens our understanding of that system. We begin to see capitalism in its entirety as a historical and social phenomenon. This perspective allows us to penetrate the appearances engendered by regarding capitalism as an isolated and discontinuous phenomenon.

Consider, for example, the exchange of equivalents that takes place between capitalist and worker. From an individual perspective, the capitalist advances value in the form of money and the labourer expends his labour-power under the control of the capitalist. Viewed historically and socially, the money advanced by the capitalist class to the working class is simply the money form of the past product of the working class. In effect, the working class purchases from the capitalist class a portion of the commodities produced by the labour of the working class. In capitalist society, the mediation of money and the commodity form of the product of labour act to obscure this process. The so-called equivalent that the capitalist brings to the exchange between capital and labour is simply the materialized past labour of the working class converted to money. Even if a capitalist originally advances capital which is the fruit of his own labour, eventually his capital becomes solely composed of value created by the labourers he employs inasmuch as the capitalist is always withdrawing profits to be spent as revenue for his own consumption. After a time, this revenue consumed privately by the capitalist, grows larger than his initial investment. Thus, all capital becomes value expropriated without an equivalent.

Regarding capitalism as a social and historical phenomenon has a profound impact on our understanding of productive and unproductive consumption. Heretofore, we were content to differentiate between productive consumption, i.e., consumption that produced surplus-value, and unproductive consumption, the personal consumption of the working class. Now we discover that capitalism incessantly reproduces the capital-wage labour relation and so must provide for the reproduction of labour-power. Seen socially, the unproductive consumption of the working class is the conversion of means of subsistence into new labour-power. In essence, when the capitalist extends a wage, he profits not only by the direct production of surplus-value but also by the fresh labour-power ensuing from the personal consumption of the labourer. The consumption of the working class becomes necessary to the continuation of capitalist production.

The constant reproduction of the relation between wage labour and capital through the exchange relations between the capitalist class and the working class causes the worker to be riveted to capital, despite the illusion of freedom generated by the act of exchange.

CHAPTER XXIV

Conversion of Surplus-Value into Capital

Hitherto we have investigated how surplus-value emanates from capital; we have now to see how capital arises from surplus-value. Employing surplus-value as capital, reconverting it into capital, is called accumulation of capital. (p. 543)

SECTION 1. CAPITALIST PRODUCTION ON A PROGRESSIVELY INCREASING SCALE. ETC.

This chapter expands our understanding of the nature of capitalism by examining the process of extended reproduction or the capitalization of surplus-value. As was noted in the last chapter, simple reproduction involves the unproductive consumption of all surplus-value by the capitalist class, in other words, the expenditure of surplus-value as revenue. Surplus-value expended as revenue does not re-enter the sphere of production and therefore does not function as capital capable of expanding its value. In the case of the conversion of surplus-value into capital, the result is an eventual augmentation of value. In both instances, a purchase is made by the capitalist, but in extended reproduction the use-value acquired (i.e., new elements of capital) is consumed productively while in simple reproduction the consumption of surplus-value is unproductive.

When the capitalist expends surplus-value productively, he accumulates capital. This accumulation involves an expansion of production both in terms of value and use-value. In order for the expansion to take place, its material elements must be available on the market. Thus, part of the annual surplus-product must include those material means of production which will exchange for surplus-value and become capitalized surplus-value. At the same time, the working class must grow to provide the necessary expansion of labour-power. Accumulation is then the reproduction of capital on a progressively increasing sale.

A concrete example of this process will enable us to understand it more clearly and, at the same time, provide us with a solution to an apparent paradox arising from the operation of the law of the exchange of equivalents. The paradox is that the laws whose operations were meant to ensure the unity of producer and property become, once labour-power is exchanged as a commodity, laws that ensure the continual separation of the labourer and property.

Suppose that a capitalist invests $10,000, $8,000 of which go to purchase means of production and $2,000 to buy labour-power; further suppose that the capitalist realizes a profit of $2,000, and that he uses the full surplus-value of $2,000 to purchase more labour-power and means of production. This $2,000 will, in turn, return him a profit of $400. As we have seen in the previous chapter, even if the first $10,000 was an initial investment that represented savings, the capitalist continually withdraws value as a portion of profit is converted into revenue for consumption. However, even leaving this process aside, the second investment of $2,000 cannot be said to represent thrift. On the contrary, what has happened is that the capitalist appropriates without an equivalent a portion of the previously materialized labour of others, and exchanges this appropriated value for an even greater quantity of living labour-power. As long as each purchase and sale corresponds to the law of exchange of equivalents, the mode of appropriation can be revolutionized without altering the rights of property. The original mode of appropriation was through labour and the exchange of commodities which were the product of the labour of their producer. The implementation of the exchange of equivalents in the context of wage labour changes the mode of appropriation to one of appropriating the labour of others through the purchase and use of the commodity labour-power.

SECTION 2. ERRONEOUS CONCEPTION, BY POLITICAL ECONOMY, OF REPRODUCTION ON A PROGRESSIVELY INCREASING SCALE

SECTION 3. SEPARATION OF SURPLUS-VALUE INTO CAPITAL AND REVENUE. THE ABSTINENCE THEORY

Classical economists preached the need to save and accumulate, since thrift was an absolute necessity in the early period of capitalist development. Indeed, the feudal nobility was criticized in part because of its parasitic and conspicuous consumption of social surplus. However, in stressing the need for productive consumption of surplus-product, classical economists, in particular Adam Smith, misrepresented accumulation as a conversion of all surplus-value into variable capital, i.e., wages. In fact, surplus-value, like the original capital, divides into constant and variable capital components. The circulation of the total social capital is the subject of the third part of Volume II and it is here that Marx traces the processes of circulation and accumulation in relation to the economy as a whole.

Surplus-value is the source of both the productive and unproductive expenditure of the capitalist class. With a given mass of surplus-value these two parts are in inverse relation. In the heroic period of capitalist accumulation, the tension between accumulation and expenditure was resolved in favour of accumulation. Accumulation was ensured both subjectively, in terms of values (e.g., of thrift) and objectively, in terms of competition and the always increasing size of capital. As capitalism developed, the moral duty of saving and thrift became the unwanted, unsought after abstinence. Abstinence demanded a reward.

Classical political economy regarded the capitalist simply as a machine for the conversion of surplus-value into capital. Further, classical economy was willing to concede that the only source of surplus-value is the labour of the working class. This formal recognition of the conflict between the working and capitalist classes could not be sustained in the face of the social upheavals brought about by industrialization. No sooner had the working class begun to rise up against the power of capital, than vulgar economy discovered a way to disguise the conflict between worker and capitalist. The disguise took the form of a theory of profit based on abstinence. Abstinence served as a justification for the reward of the capitalist. As Marx points out, the role of abstainer is tied to ownership of capital, the existence of capital. Given a different mode of production, it is possible to envisage expanded reproduction without the capitalist abstainer.

SECTION 4. CIRCUMSTANCES THAT, INDEPENDENTLY OF THE PROPORTIONAL DIVISION OF SURPLUS-VALUE INTO CAPITAL AND REVENUE, DETERMINE THE AMOUNT OF ACCUMULATION. ETC.

Assuming a fixed proportional division between revenue and capitalized surplus-value, all factors that lead to an expansion of the total mass of surplus-value make accelerated accumulation possible. Marx proceeds to delineate various means of accelerating accumulation with a given division of surplus-value into savings and revenue. In practice, an important part is played by lowering wages below the value of labour-power. This reduction in the consumption fund of the working class is a clear source of additional surplus-value and, hence, of accelerated accumulation. Increasing the intensity of labour is another fruitful area for the expansion of capital. An increase in the hours of labour does not require proportionately increased investment in the instruments of labour and thus permits greater relative expenditure of capital for labour-power, the source of surplus-value. In a similar manner, surplus-value is augmented by increasing the intensity of labour in industries where labour and nature directly interact. Here constant capital remains small because the subject of labour is not a product of previous labour but rather is provided by nature. In combining labour-power and nature, capital acquires an ability to expand beyond its apparent limits.

The development of the social productivity of labour is an important source of accelerated accumulation. In technical terms, an ever-increasing means of production is available for accumulation. The concomitant development of relative surplus-value through a reduction in the value of labour-power is also a powerful lever for increased accumulation. Because elements of constant capital are cheapened by productivity gains, the replacement of constant capital frees capital for new investment. Thus, advances in science and technology give capital the power to expand beyond its original magnitude.

The overall process of accumulation leads to an absolute as

well as relative increase in constant capital. The ability of labour-power to transfer value means that the greater the amount of functioning constant capital in relation to labour, the greater the value transferred by a given quantity of labour-power. Thus we see that the conditions of labour furnished by nature and society render capital accumulation relatively independent of the magnitude of invested capital.

SECTION 5. THE SO-CALLED LABOUR FUND

The appearance that at any given moment the quantity of capital is fixed, provides bourgeois political economists with support for a theory that the wage fund (the portion of society's production employed for workers' subsistence) is fixed, unalterable by class struggle. Marx refutes this argument and points out its obviously self-serving quality. At bottom, the idea of a labour fund represents a justification for the repression and restriction of trade union activity.

CHAPTER XXV

The General Law of Capitalist Accumulation

The labouring population therefore produces, along with the accumulation of capital produced by it, the means by which it itself is made relatively superfluous, is turned into a relative surplus-population . . . (p. 591)

SECTION 1. THE INCREASED DEMAND FOR LABOUR-POWER THAT ACCOMPANIES ACCUMULATION, THE COMPOSITION OF CAPITAL REMAINING THE SAME

As Marx states at its beginning, the present chapter is concerned with the effects of the accumulation of capital upon the working class. The concept of the composition of capital is central to Marx's analysis here as well as to topics considered later in *Capital*.

Earlier in the text, we established that capital advanced for production is divided into two constituents: a variable component which purchases labour-power; and a constant component paid out for material means of production. The relation between these two components is termed the "value composition" of capital. The value composition finds its basis in the technical nature of the productive process. Given a particular mode of production, a certain proportion is established between material means of production and living labour employed in the production of a commodity. This relationship between the mass of means of production and the quantity of labour necessary to set them in motion is called the "technical composition" of capital. Thus, the technical composition of capital is grounded in use-values. The values of the two components of the technical composition of capital serve to define its value composition. Marx introduces the term "organic composition" of capital to emphasize the dependence of the value composition on the technical composition. In general, the organic composition of capital is expressed as the ratio of the value of constant to that of variable capital. Therefore, a capital with a "high" organic composition is one which contains a relatively large constant capital constituent.

There are variations in the organic composition of capital across the spheres of production in society and, indeed, there is also variation within spheres. In this chapter, Marx attends to the average organic composition of the "total social capital." The concepts of the total social capital and its organic composition reappear prominently later in *Capital.* For the purposes of the first section of this chapter, the assumption is made that the organic composition of capital does not change with the process of capital accumulation. This assumption, relaxed in the remainder of the chapter, serves to simplify the initial analysis. An unchanging (as opposed to increasing) organic composition of capital is also, as we shall see, the situation most favourable to the working class.

In extended reproduction, that is, the process of capital accumulation, a part of surplus-value is capitalized and reinvested in production. If the organic composition of capital remains unaltered, the proportions in which this surplus-value is divided into new constant and variable components is the same as the division of the original capital. Thus, the demand for labour increases at the same rate as the accumulation of capital. Finally, if, as is likely, the supply of labour increases more slowly than accumulation, the process of accumulation itself will result in a rise in wages. We shall see in a moment, however, that this process is self-limiting.

In the chapter on simple reproduction, Marx indicated how the wage relation serves to reproduce itself: the worker must continue to sell his labour-power to the capitalist. Extended reproduction not only reproduces the wage relation but produces it on an ever more extensive scale. Moreover, the increasing subjugation of labour to capital is not inconsistent with a rise in wages, so long as the increase in wages is insufficient to interfere with the process of accumulation itself. Indeed, wage gains can never permanently hinder accumulation. For if accumulation slackens, so does the rate of increase in the demand for labour and, with it, the cause of higher wages.

Marx makes the important point, elaborated in the following sections, that the relation between the supply of and demand for labour (and, thus, the level of wages) is the product of the rate of accumulation of capital. The former is the effect, the latter, the cause, not vice-versa. Furthermore, since the rate of accumulation depends upon the division of the working day into paid and unpaid labour (expressed in wages and surplus-value, respectively), the relation between accumulation and wages resolves itself into the relation of the unpaid to the paid labour furnished by the working class. Here, Marx is critical of the notion (e.g., propounded by Malthus) that the level of wages is determined according to a natural law by the size and rate of increase of the labouring population. Marx's analysis shows that the demand for labour is dependent upon the accumulation of capital. This analysis and critique is extended in section 3, below.

SECTION 2. RELATIVE DIMINUTION OF THE VARIABLE PART OF CAPITAL SIMULTANEOUSLY WITH THE PROGRESS OF ACCUMULATION AND OF THE CONCENTRATION THAT ACCOMPANIES IT

The assumption, adopted temporarily in the previous section, that the organic composition of capital is fixed as accumulation takes place, is not realistic. For, as accumulation progresses, capitalism comes to revolutionize the mode of production and thereby increases the productivity of labour. This increased productivity of labour exercises a profound effect upon the technical composition of capital, increasing the mass of means of production in relation to the labour required to set the means of production in motion. The origin of the effect is twofold: first, the amount of raw material processed by a given amount of labour increases dramatically; secondly, productivity gains are themselves dependent upon vast extension of the instruments of labour. The value composition of capital increases as a consequence of its growing technical composition, though the value composition does not increase proportionately. Increases in productivity, after all, cheapen the elements of constant capital.

In sum, then, the variable portion of capital grows more slowly than its constant component. Consequently, the demand for labour increases at a rate which is slower than the rate of accumulation of capital.

The concentration of a certain amount of capital in the hands of individual capitalists is one of the prerequisites of capitalist production. The historical process by which this original concentration of capital takes place, a process which Marx calls "primitive accumulation," is described toward the end of Volume I. Once the basis for capitalist production exists, the accumulation of capital brings about its further concentration which, in turn, fosters the continued development of capitalist production.

Two opposed processes govern the general growth of social capital. On the one hand, individual capitals proliferate as old capital is divided or gives rise to new. On the other hand, it is increasingly the case that formerly separate capitals are combined or centralized. Marx takes pains to differentiate between the concentration of capital, the product of extended reproduction, and its centralization, the combination of previously independent capitals. The latter process represents a redistribution of capital rather than its extension and is accomplished by the absorption of one capital by another or by the formation of joint stock companies. Centralization is brought about primarily by competition and the workings of the credit system, factors which are discussed at length later in *Capital*. Together, concentration and centralization of capital serve to increase the scale of production and, thus, to increase the organic composition of capital and the productivity of labour.

The foregoing analysis established that capitalized surplus-value is invested at an ever-increasing organic composition. As a consequence, we have seen that the demand for labour grows more slowly than accumulation. However, in the process of reproduction not only a portion of surplus-value but also constant and variable capital re-enter production. Since these elements of old capital are reinvested under new conditions, including a higher organic composition of capital, part of the labour employed by the old capital becomes superfluous to it.

SECTION 3. PROGRESSIVE PRODUCTION OF A RELATIVE SURPLUS-POPULATION OR INDUSTRIAL RESERVE ARMY

Population theorists such as Malthus explain the poverty of the working class on the basis of an abstract or general "law" of population, a law not specific to the capitalist mode of production. According to these theorists, the expansion of means of subsistence, taking the form of high wages under capitalism, produces a population increase which, in turn, exhausts the means of subsistence (i.e., under capitalism, produces a fall in wages). Marx, on the other hand, does not derive a general law of population applicable to all societies; rather, he develops the relationship between the population of the working class and the growth of capital within the specific context of the capitalist mode of production. In the course of his exposition, Marx produces a devastating critique of the Malthusian argument.

We have established that the change in the organic composition of capital which accompanies accumulation implies that the demand for labour grows more slowly than accumulation itself. In particular spheres of production, this process is not smooth and even, but at the level of the total social capital it is more or less continuous. The product of the decreasing proportion of variable capital is unemployment: what Marx terms "relative surplus-population" — relative, because the surplus is in relation to the demand of capital for labour. At times, and in certain industries, the creation of relative surplus-population is clear, when technological innovation results in the dismissal of labourers. In other instances, the process is more subtle, when employment expands more slowly than it otherwise would under a constant organic composition of capital. The expansion of capital, based upon the surplus-value produced by the working class, is therefore the source of relative surplus-population. The surplus-population which results from the expansion of capital also serves to further the process of capital accumulation.

Modern industry is characterized by a business cycle of roughly a decade in length. Marx develops a theory of the business cycle and economic crises in Volume II of *Capital*. Here, however, he notes that the demand for labour is highest during the expansionary portion of the cycle. The surplus-population "set free" by the expansion of capital provides an "industrial reserve army" available to capital when the demand for labour is high. If the working-class population were only large enough to meet the average needs of capital, there would be a shortage of labour during the peak periods of the business cycle. Therefore, Marx's theory of capital accumulation and his theory of the business cycle are intimately related.

Capital can increase its command of labour not only by increasing the number of labourers employed but also by raising the intensity of labour, by increasing the length of the working day, and by substituting cheaper labour (unskilled workers, women and children) for more expensive. These processes additionally serve to increase the size of the industrial reserve army. Hence, we encounter the anomalous situation of simultaneous overwork and unemployment.

Wages, the price of labour, are determined by the supply of and demand for labour and, hence, by the size of the reserve army of the unemployed (the excess of supply over demand). As we have seen, the number of unemployed rises and falls with the phases of the business cycle. These changes are relatively independent of the absolute size of the working class population. As we mentioned earlier, Malthus and his followers attribute wage changes to variations in the growth rate of the population: when wages are high, the birth rate rises, eventually increasing the size of the labouring population; the increased supply of labour causes a fall in its price which, in turn, results in a decreased birth rate; and so on. As Marx points out, this argument is specious. The period of variation of wages is, in actuality, the period of the business cycle: roughly ten years. A generation would have to elapse before an increase in the birth rate were reflected in a larger supply of labourers. Thus, the surplus-population of the unemployed is relative not absolute: that is, relative to the demand for labour governed by the business cycle and the growth of capital.

Marx goes on to argue that the Malthusians confuse the mechanisms which regulate wages and employment in particular spheres of production with those which control the movement of wages in the economy as a whole, incorrectly reasoning that the latter are similar to the former. When the demand for labour is especially high in a particular sphere of production, wages in the sphere rise. As a consequence, labourers are attracted to that sphere, increasing the local supply of labour and causing wages there to fall. Political economists such as Malthus draw an invalid analogy between the movement of labourers among spheres of production and changes in the size of the working class and employment as a whole. As noted above, the general supply of labour cannot respond to relatively short-term changes in demand.

In summary, the existence of a reserve army of labourers places constraints on the movement of wages occasioned by the law of supply and demand. The tendency of capital accumulation to increase the demand for labour is offset by the unemployment that results from the changes in the composition of capital which are also the product of the process of accumulation.

SECTION 4. DIFFERENT FORMS OF THE RELATIVE SURPLUS-POPULATION. THE GENERAL LAW OF CAPITALISTIC ACCUMULATION

Every unemployed or partially employed worker is a member of the relative surplus-population. Marx differentiates three strata of the surplus-population. Briefly, the first of these strata is termed the "floating," and consists of labourers who are alternately hired and discharged as a consequence of technological change and capital accumulation in modern industry. The floating component of the surplus-population is also recruited from the ranks of child labourers who lose their jobs when they reach maturity. The mechanization of agriculture produces an absolute (not merely a relative) decrease in the demand for agricultural labour. Agricultural labourers consequently migrate to urban areas when employment opportunities present themselves. While they remain in rural areas, these workers comprise the "latent" component of relative surplus-population. The third and lowest stratum of the surplus-population is the "stagnant," consisting of individuals who are employed only infrequently.

We have seen that the development of capital accumulation entails the production of relative surplus-population. Put another way: although the productivity of labour and the accumulation of capital grow more quickly than population, these same processes ensure that employment grows more slowly than population. Consequently, the subjugation of labour to capital increases as accumulation proceeds. This is what Marx terms the "absolute (i.e., abstract) general law of capitalist accumulation."

SECTION 5. ILLUSTRATIONS OF THE GENERAL LAW OF CAPITALIST ACCUMULATION

As noted above, Marx's stated purpose in this chapter is to examine how capitalist accumulation affects the working class. The material in the final section of this chapter, dealing with sanitation, health, housing and nutrition of workers — in short, with their conditions of life — serves to illustrate the theoretical material developed earlier in the chapter. Furthermore, these illustrations supplement previous descriptions (for example, in Marx's discussion of the length of the working day) of the effects of capitalist development on working conditions.

The detailed illustrative nature of the material in this section makes it difficult to summarize. However, we offer the following general remarks: First, most of the material pertains to England in the period from 1846 to 1866. Marx notes that he chose to examine England because of the advanced development of capitalism in that country, and the years 1846-1866 because of the dramatic capital accumulation which took place during this period. Secondly, the example of Ireland, during roughly the same time span, serves to illustrate that surplus-population is not absolute but rather must be measured relative to the needs of capital. Thus, at a time when Ireland was losing population to famine and emigration, it continued to be over-populated in relation to the requirements of a progressively capitalized agriculture.

PART VIII

The So-Called Primitive Accumulation

CHAPTER XXVI

The Secret of Primitive Accumulation

> *The so-called primitive accumulation, therefore, is nothing else than the historical process of divorcing the producer from the means of production. (p. 668)*

In the course of the exposition, Marx has demonstrated both the logical and the historical course of the development of capitalism. In Part II, he examined the transformation of money into capital and delineated the preconditions necessary for the occurrence of this processs. In the movement from C-M-C to M-C-M, it was absolutely essential that the capitalist entrepreneur be able to purchase labour-power as a commodity. It was the existence of labour-power as a commodity that enabled money to become capital.

It follows from the logical conditions for capitalism that in studying the genesis of capitalism the crucial process is the one that involves the separation of the producer from the means of production. The dissolution of the feudal mode of production set free the elements which would constitute the basis for capitalist development. Thus, the demise of feudalism transformed the serf into an independent commodity producer. Once the serf was freed from the obligations of feudalism, only his ownership of the means of production stood in the way of the development of wage-labour, that is, the buying and selling of labour-power as a commodity.

The process of primitive accumulation is precisely the process of the separation of agrarian small producers from their means of production, the land. Once capitalism was established, it ensured the continuation of this process through the commodity form of the product of labour. Furthermore, the expanded reproduction of capitalist relations takes place due to the increase in the productivity of social labour under capitalism and the consequent concentration and centralization of capital. As long as exchange is promoted, economic competition between a more productive and a less productive mode of production will result in the destruction or transformation of the small producers.

The industrial bourgeoisie, developing within feudalism, waged a long and bitter struggle for social and political power with the feudal nobility and the guild masters. This epochal battle, stretching over centuries, resulted in the victory of the bourgeoisie and the consequent liberation of the capitalist mode of production from the restrictions of feudalism.

In studying the transition from feudalism to capitalism and the crucial transformation of the dominant form of extraction of surplus labour from rent to surplus-value, the separation of the direct producer from the means of production is the most important aspect. In subsequent chapters, Marx presents a concrete instance of the course of this development by examining the history of England. While individual countries show substantial variations, the general result is everywhere the same: labour-power appears as a commodity, making possible the production of surplus-value and the expansion of capital.

CHAPTER XXVII

Expropriation of the Agricultural Population from the Land

The spoilation of the church's property, the fraudulent alienation of the State domains, the robbery of the common lands, the usurpation of feudal and clan property, and its transformation into modern private property under circumstances of reckless terrorism, were just so many idyllic methods of primitive accumulation. (p. 685)

The dissolution of the system of feudal agriculture led to the domination of production by small peasant proprietors in late 15th century England. These peasants exercised de facto ownership and control of their land despite the continued existence of surface feudal titles. In order for England to undergo the process of capitalist development, the free peasant proprietors had to be separated from the land. Separation from the land would make the former peasants dependent upon the sale of their labour-power in order to ensure their existence. This result was the product of a six-part movement encompassing all the forms of land ownership.

Chronologically, the first important contribution to the formation of a pool of wage-labour was the destruction of the system of feudal retainers. This process was pursued by the crown seeking to create an absolute monarchy by weakening the power of the nobility. Far exceeding the first step in importance was the forcible eviction of peasants and the usurpation of common lands by the nobility in its rush to convert agricultural land to sheep farming. The expropriation of the peasantry by the nobility that emerged from the period of the great feudal wars completely overrode the traditional rights of the feudal period. This policy was so revolutionary in its effects and implications that the monarchy of the period sought to restrain and offset its impact.

The English Reformation and consequent seizure and redistribution of church property had an important effect on the size of the newly formed proletariat. Hereditary sub-tenants were driven en masse from the newly-constituted private property. Indeed, the whole network of rights and obligations of the church lands was overthrown with one stroke. Inasmuch as these rights and obligations constituted the bulwark of the old moral economy, this economy was effectively abolished.

The class of yeoman farmers, the backbone of agriculture, was destroyed through both economic and political means. Politically, the landed proprietors abolished feudal tenure and appropriated the rights of modern private property for themselves. Subsequently, the nascent bourgeoisie, the new landed aristocracy and the new bankocracy created a political alliance through the distribution of state lands at exceedingly low prices. It was these lands, together with those confiscated from the church, that formed the estates of the 19th century oligarchy.

The appropriation of communal property, resisted by legislation for over 150 years, was legalized in the 18th century by Acts for Enclosures of Commons, permitting the landlords to acquire the people's property. The appropriation of this property served to increase the scale of agriculture, making possible the establishment of capitalist farms.

Finally, the process known as the "clearing of the estates" brought to a conclusion the separation of the direct producer from his means of production. In Scotland, the entire system of clan property was dismantled through the appropriation of title by the hereditary chief of the clan. For example, the Duchess of Sutherland ejected 15,000 peasants from the land, converting her property into sheep farms. Together, these various processes created a capitalized agriculture along with a potential urban proletariat.

CHAPTER XXVIII

Bloody Legislation Against the Expropriated, from the End of the 15th Century. Forcing Down of Wages by Acts of Parliament

The bourgeoisie, at its rise, wants and uses the power of the state to "regulate" wages, i.e., to force them within the limits suitable for surplus-value making, to lengthen the working-day and to keep the labourer himself in the normal degree of dependence. (p. 689)

The slow pace of accumulation during the early period of capitalist development was unable to provide employment for the masses of small producers who were expelled from the land. The result was a great increase in vagabondage and banditry, as displaced peasants struggled for survival in an increasingly hostile world.

The increase in displaced peasants called forth a continuous stream of repressive legislation from the state. The legislation performed a dual function. On the one hand, it attempted to deal with the problem of vagabondage, while on the other, it served as a punitive legislative weapon that enforced the new work disciplines of capitalism.

Once it is widely established, the capitalist system generates the conditions of its continued existence and reproduction. However, in the period of the genesis of capitalism, the political intervention of the state is required to keep wages low, lengthen the working day, and shackle the labourer to capital. Legislation was especially important as soon as capitalist development acquired a degree of momentum. At that time, the organic composition of capital was low and accumulation, for a large part, resolved itself into wages, or variable capital. This, together with the existence of an independent peasantry and the guild organizations, acted to shield the newly-emerging working class from the full force of capitalist exploitation. In this early period, the working class was able to extract a relatively high price for its formal subjection to capital. This situation called for state intervention on behalf of the nascent capitalist class, intervention which took the form of restrictions on wages. The resulting legislation remained on the books long after the development of capitalism had rendered it redundant. The history of state economic intervention in the service of the capitalist class makes a mockery of the claim of the 19th and 20th century bourgeoisie that state interference in the market place is a blow against freedom and economic rationality.

CHAPTER XXIX

Genesis of the Capitalist Farmer

> *As far, however, as concerns the genesis of the farmer, we can, so to say, put our hand on it, because it is a slow process evolving through many centuries. (p. 694)*

Having sketched the historical process that brought the working class into existence, Marx now turns his attention to the complementary question of the genesis of the capitalist class. The evolution of the capitalist farmer was a slow process, unfolding as it did through several centuries. The second half of the 14th century witnessed the emergence of a type of farmer who employed wage labour but remained dependent on the landlord for his means of production. Slowly and imperceptibly, this stratum acquired the capital to provide its own means of production.

This group of farmers was particularly well placed to appropriate the gains of the agricultural revolution of the latter 15th and the 16th centuries. The principal mechanism bringing about the appropriation was long-term leases in a period of rising prices. The class of capitalist farmers developed at the expense of both the agricultural labourers and the great landlords. By the end of the 16th century, England's capitalist farmer class was particularly vigorous and healthy. It was in a strong position to benefit from the further development of commercialized agriculture that resulted in the creation of the home market.

CHAPTER XXX

Reaction of the Agricultural Revolution on Industry. Creation of the Home-Market for Industrial Capital

The expropriation and eviction of a part of the agricultural population not only set free for industrial capital, the labourers, their means of subsistence, and material for labour; it also created the home-market. (p. 699)

The separation of town and country under the capitalist mode of production had important implications for the development of the market. Prior to this separation, the independent agrarian producer laboured to produce use-values such as agricultural and non-agricultural means of subsistence. Expelled from the land which constituted the means of production required for the production of agricultural means of subsistence, he was at the same time deprived of the wherewithal to produce use-values such as clothing.

Thus, markets for specialized commercial agricultural production and for the products of industrial capital were by-products of the rural expulsions. These processes culminated in the creation of the home market and the destruction of rural domestic industry. They began during the period of manufacture; however, as we discovered earlier, manufacture rested on an incomplete and inadequate handicraft foundation. Therefore, we witness the periodic re-creation of domestic industry on an ever-shrinking scale. Modern industry completed the rationalization of agriculture and the resulting separation of agriculture and rural domestic industry.

CHAPTER XXXI

Genesis of the Industrial Capitalist

> *If money ... "comes into the world with a congenital blood-stain on one cheek," capital comes dripping from head to foot, from every pore, with blood and dirt. (pp. 711-712)*

In contrast to the evolutionary development of the capitalist farmer, the industrial capitalist emerged in hothouse fashion. Prior to the development of the capitalist mode of production, capital existed in two forms: usurer's capital and merchant capital. It was the transformation of these two forms that allowed the development of industrial capital to proceed so rapidly.

Commercial and usurer's capital grew enormously as a result of the colonial-mercantile system. Indeed, the bulk of merchant profit was extracted through trade or outright plunder in the colonial countries. During the manufacturing period, it was precisely in the development of the colonial and commercial system that the superiority of certain nation states was established. This result is in contrast to the modern period in which industrial superiority is the key to national power.

Primitive accumulation produced by the profits of the colonial system was augmented by the development of the public debt. At one stroke, money that could find no employment as capital by its owner became financial capital, capital capable of undergoing the circuit M-M′. Furthermore, the state debt provided a basis for the development of quasi-official national banks that acquired powers of expansion undreamed of by private capital.

The development of the public debt brought about the necessity of the modern taxation system, a system implemented in order to fund the debt. The taxation system became a powerful means for expropriating the lower-middle classes and thereby producing a centralization of capital that was favourable to more extended accumulation. The system of protection was an additional mechanism to bring about the same result. Thus, the network of the colonial system, the public debt, heavy taxation, protection and commercial wars forms the basis for the development of modern industry. In turn, modern industry greatly reinforces these features of society.

CHAPTER XXXII

Historical Tendency of Capitalist Accumulation

Along with the constantly diminishing number of the magnates of capital ... grows the mass of misery, oppression, slavery, degradation, exploitation; but with this too grows the revolt of the working class ... (p. 715)

In this chapter, Marx provides a brief sketch of the actual course of historical development and links this movement to a general principle of societal change. Rather than presenting a complete analysis, this section merely serves to introduce the complex question of the nature and causes of the transition from capitalism to socialism.

As we have seen in the preceding chapters, the central process of primitive accumulation, the creation of a class of wage labourers, resolves itself into a series of forcible methods resulting in the expropriation of independent commodity producers. The emerging capitalist class, both in agriculture and in industry, used the state to dismantle obstacles to the development of the productive power of social labour. Political action served to ensure the victory of the political economy of the bourgeoisie. This historical period was the prelude to the development of industrial capitalism.

Once capitalism is firmly established as a mode of production within a social formation, it is no longer necessary for it to rely on the machinery of the state. The demise of small private property is produced by the socialization of the forces of production through the development of the immanent laws of capitalism. This process is the concentration and centralization of capital which was described in an earlier section. Essentially, more and more capital becomes monopolized by fewer and fewer capitalists. The contradictory movement of private property in the development of capitalism is striking. Beginning from the identity of private property and capital, the inexorable laws of capitalist development produce socially developed means of production. This movement takes place within the existing framework of private property. Development continues until a point is reached where the further evolution of the forces of production is blocked by capitalist relations of production. At this point, the objective preconditions exist for a working-class social revolution.

CHAPTER XXXIII

The Modern Theory of Colonization

The capitalist mode of production and accumulation, and therefore capitalist private property, have for their fundamental condition the annihilation of self-earned private property . . . (p. 724)

Capitalism, appearing to rest on the sanctity of private property, in the final analysis is built upon the abolition of individual private property. This conclusion was not obvious in the 19th century, for the process of primitive accumulation had taken place centuries before. Capitalism, triumphant, obscures the means of its triumph. There is, however, one place where the opposition between independent, small private property and the development of capitalism remains clear: in the white settler colonies of the Empire. Here, the basic incompatability of these two modes of production, capitalism and petty commodity production, is forcefully asserted. Indeed, the impediment to the development of the colonies was so profound that the English colonial office was forced to devise a plan whose premise was precisely the opposition between the two modes of production.

The foreign office discovered that if no wage labour were available, the development of capitalism became impossible. Regardless of the level of technical advancement, capital remains a social relation and not an object. In the absence of the social relations between worker and capitalist mediated by wages it is impossible for capital accumulation to take place. In response to the scarcity of labour in the colonies, an economist by the name of Wakefield formulated a plan artificially to raise the price of land. As a consequence, every settler would be forced to work as a labourer for a number of years in order to acquire enough money to purchase the land required for independent commodity production. In other words, all of the processes that have been described by Marx in this part of Volume I of *Capital*, such as separation of the labourer from means of production, development of the internal market, and the separation of agriculture and industry, cannot be realized in the colonies because of the existence of private property in land. The existence of free land acts as a barrier to the formation of a pool of wage labour required for the expansion of capital.

Wakefield's proposal was outstripped by events. All it succeeded in accomplishing was diverting immigration to the United States. Its importance rests not on its success or failure as a policy, but on the principle it propounded: that capitalism has as its fundamental basis the destruction of independent commodity production.

PART I

Commodities and Money

CHAPTER I

Commodities

> *Value, therefore, does not stalk about with a label describing what it is. It is value, rather, that converts every product into a social hieroglyphic. (p. 79)*

Although it would be an exaggeration to say that the three volumes of *Capital* are an unfolding of the material in the first chapters of Volume I, the material in these chapters, particularly in Chapter I, provides the logical foundation upon which the rest of *Capital* is erected. This foundation is both substantive and methodological.

We return, then, to Chapter I in the expectation that the material will be illuminated by the remainder of the book and with the hope that this material will, in turn, reflect light on the rest. At this time, it would be useful to reread the summaries of Sections 1 ("The Two Factors of a Commodity: Use-Value and Value") and 2 ("The Two-Fold Character of the Labour Embodied in Commodities") of Chapter I, since we shall not repeat them here.

SECTION 3. THE FORM OF VALUE OR EXCHANGE-VALUE

On first reading, Section 3 of Chapter I appears overly pedantic. However, we should appreciate that Marx struggles with difficult ideas in this section and deals with topics which are the subject of misunderstanding and mystification. Aside from developing the concept of exchange-value and its relation to value, Marx makes a historical point about the development of commodity exchange, provides a basis for an understanding of money (a topic which is pursued in Chapter III and later in *Capital*), and introduces the subject of the next section on "commodity fetishism."

We have seen that the value of a commodity is the amount of socially necessary labour expended in its production. Value, however, is not something which is observed directly, but manifests itself only when commodities enter into relations of exchange with one another. Exchange-value, then, is the expression, or phenomenal form, of value.

To illuminate the distinction between value and its form, exchange-value, Marx develops an analogy between value and weight. To paraphrase, suppose that we had before us objects of two different sorts, coats and shoes, say, and wished to determine their relative weights. We could make this comparison by placing the objects in the pans of a scale and observing the amount of one object that balances the other. We might find that six shoes are the equivalent in weight of one coat.

This operation is analogous to what Marx terms the elementary or accidental form of value, i.e., barter. Here, one commodity exchanges for a definite quantity of another; for simplicity, suppose that one coat exchanges for six shoes. Just as in the weight analogy, where the weight of the coat found its expression in its weight equivalent, the six shoes, so in the elementary form of value, the value of the coat finds its expression in its value equivalent, the six shoes. In each case, the weight or value of the coat is expressed relative to the weight or value of the shoes. The shoes, on the other hand, function as an equivalent or standard, an embodiment of weight (in the one case) or value (in the other). In Marx's terminology, the expression of value has two forms or poles: the relative form (the coat) whose value is expressed, and the equivalent form (the shoes) in which value is expressed. The equivalent form of value is peculiar in the following sense (among others): a particular commodity, a use-value, becomes the expression of an abstract property of commodities, their value. Similarly, in the weight analogy, a particular object serves as a standard of an abstract, or general, property of objects, their weight.

Once commodity exchange has progressed to a certain stage, a particular commodity (e.g., a coat) exchanges in various proportions with many other commodities. Each of these other commodities (in their respective proportions) is the value equivalent of the single commodity, the coat. This is the total or expanded form of value, a form which relates the value of one commodity to the values of all others.

Now, since the value relation is an equivalence relation, it can be reversed: just as the coat expresses its value in the shoes, by exchanging for them in a particular proportion, so the shoes express their value in the coat. Reversing the expanded form of value yields the general form: the expression of the values of all commodities (save one) by their exchange relations to (that is, the proportions in which they exchange for) a particular commodity.

Returning to the analogy of value to weight; in determining the weights of objects it is usual to compare them with a standard set of weights, for example, of lead or iron. These standard weights function as a general weight equivalent. In this role, they are analogous to the money commodity, which functions as the standard general form of value.

We have pursued the analogy between weight and value in order to explain the structure of Marx's exposition. However, as Marx notes, the analogy is limited in the following sense: while weight is a physical property of objects, value is social in nature. Through the medium of exchange, governed by value relations, individual producers interact with one another. It is the nature of this interaction and the manner in which it appears on the surface of society, which concerns Marx in the following section.

SECTION 4. THE FETISHISM OF COMMODITIES AND THE SECRET THEREOF

To fetishize an object is to attribute mystical properties to it. The fetishism of commodities entails a misunderstanding of their social nature, the mistaken idea that the value of a commodity is an intrinsic property of the commodity as an object.

In commodity production, private individuals interact with each other not directly but indirectly through the commodities that they produce and exchange. In fact, their social relations are rendered even more indirect when exchange is mediated by the agency of the money commodity.

Although the relations among producers underlie the exchange relations of commodities, at the surface of society only the exchange relations are visible. These exchange relations are not unreal, they are merely superficial, and they are explained (not explained away) by social relations.

Marx notes that value relations are not necessarily obscured in all forms of society. Starting with a non-social example, an isolated producer (Robinson Crusoe serves as an illustration) necessarily accounts for his various productive activities in terms of labour time expended in their pursuit. Likewise, social relations among classes in feudal society are direct, not mediated, and therefore do not take on a confusing form. The division of labour in a family is also of a directly social nature and is similarly unobscured. Finally, in a socialist community, the social relations of production and distribution are clear as well. Each individual contributes to the total social product and consumes a portion of it.

Vulgar economy treats only appearances, rather than investigating the relations underlying these appearances. Hence, the vulgar economist fails to see the social relations underlying the exchange of commodities and, instead, attributes "mystical properties" to the commodities themselves. The value of a commodity is seen as a property of the object itself and thus value becomes confused with use-value.

CHAPTER II

Exchange

The historical progress and extension of exchanges develops the contrast, latent in commodities, between use-value and value. (p. 90)

Marx has defined a commodity as a product of labour that is produced in order to be exchanged. Since commodities are inanimate objects, their exchange presupposes the intervention of people. Thus, relations of commodity exchange are fundamentally social relations. In *Capital,* Marx abstracts from the particular characteristics of individuals: individuals appear as personifications of underlying economic roles and relationships. In later chapters the capitalist is treated as capital personified, and the individual worker appears as the personification of wage labour. In the present discussion, individuals entering into relations of commodity exchange are viewed as interacting solely through their commodity products. Marx's method of abstraction serves to throw economic relations into relief, where they can be examined and dissected.

A commodity owner exchanges his commodity when it has no immediate use-value for him. His ultimate goal is the acquisition of a commodity for which he has a use. Since this acquisition requires exchange, the seller of a commodity must realize its value before he can realize a use-value. On the other hand, a commodity must function as a use-value for its purchaser in order for him to be motivated to buy it. In this manner, exchange combines a private and a social moment that reflects the opposition internal to commodities: the polarity of value and use-value.

The social nature of the act of exchange requires some socially recognized medium that will allow it to extend beyond barter. This socially recognized medium or equivalent is a commodity the same as any other; however, it acquires the additional use-value of being the money commodity. In money, value finds an independent form.

Exchange without the mediation of money is called barter. Here, two commodites are exchanged directly. Although the proportions at which commodities exchange are originally random, as exchange develops these relative magnitudes become fixed by custom. At the barter stage, value does not have an independent form. The independent form of value, money, is a product of the extension and regulation of exchange, a process which continues until exchange reaches a stage of development that specifies certain natural properties of the universal value equivalent: uniformity of quality and simplicity of quantification. Gold and silver have these properties. Thus, the particular commodity, gold, the universal equivalent, acquires a new use-value: the use of being money. As in the case of all commodities, the value of gold is determined by the labour time required for its production. Gold, then, is simply a commodity. The money-form is the expression of the value relations among all commodities in terms of a single commodity. The money-form of gold is simply the form under which social relations of exchange, based upon the exchange of value equivalents, manifest themselves. Therefore, the riddle posed by the sudden appearance of money is not a new riddle, but simply a reformulation of the problem posed by the exchange of commodities generally. That Marx regards the two as equivalent is clear from the title to the next chapter, "Money or the Circulation of Commodities."

CHAPTER III

Money, or the Circulation of Commodities

It is because all commodities, as values, are realized human labour, and therefore commensurable, that their values can be measured by one and the same special commodity, and the latter to be converted into the common measure of their values, i.e., into money. (p. 97)

SECTION 1. THE MEASURE OF VALUES

The chief function of money is to provide an independent and material expression of value. It is this function that renders gold the money commodity. Thus, money is the phenomenal form assumed by the labour time that is the determinant of value inherent in commodities.

The monetary expression of value is price, which is a purely ideal or mental form, depending as it does on imagined exchange. It is possible to use imaginary money as a measure of value, for example. When a potential seller quotes a price for his commodity, he establishes an imagined relationship between a quantity of the commodity and a definite quantity of gold. Money also serves as a standard of price as distinct from its function as a measure of value. As a measure of value, money is the socially recognized incarnation of human labour that serves to convert values into prices. As a standard of price, money establishes a correspondence between a particular unit of currency (e.g., the dollar) and a specific quantity of gold. These two functions are autonomous.

SECTION 2. THE MEDIUM OF CIRCULATION

Materially, the process of exchange is the social circulation of objects, a process which is brought about through the metamorphoses of commodities in sale and purchase. As we have seen, exchange is at once a social and a private activity. The development of the differentiation of commodities and money expresses this contradiction. Money embodies the social aspect of commodities, their exchange-value, while the commodities themselves are characterized by particular use-values. The differentiation of commodities and money, therefore, corresponds to the dual nature of commodities themselves.

Exchange can be divided into the two acts of selling and buying. The first act converts a commodity into money, while the other reconverts money into a commodity. The exchange of commodities manifests the transformation of value from the commodity form to the money form and back to the commodity form. This process of transformation is represented by the "formula" C-M-C.

The first metamorphosis is C-M, or the transformation of a commodity into money. Throughout the first and second volumes of *Capital*, Marx makes the simplifying assumption that commodities exchange at their value. However, a discrepancy between "social value" and "individual value" is possible, and Marx identifies some of the mechanisms that can serve to bring about such a discrepancy. "Social value" is the value established by socially necessary labour time, while "individual value" is the amount of labour time contained in a particular commodity product. Circumstances such as changes in the socially necessary labour time required for the reproduction of an article or a misallocation of society's global labour time due to the anarchy of production can result in differences between individual and social value. In the first instance, for example, the value of a commodity will fall if the labour time necessary for its production decreases. Under these circumstances, a commodity can be reproduced in less time than was originally required for its production. In the second instance, for example, if a commodity is produced in a supply which exceeds demand, producers of that commodity will be unable to realize its full individual value.

Gold has both an ideal and a real existence as money. As ideal money, gold is the measure of value and standard of price. As real money, gold actually changes place with commodities and becomes the embodiment of their value. When commodities are metamorphosed into money through sale, they transform themselves into socially recognized, homogeneous human labour.

At the same time as C-M takes place, its opposite, M-C, takes place as well. As one individual converts his commodity into money, another must convert his money into a commodity. The second metamorphosis, M-C, like the first, implies its opposite, C-M. When a buyer concludes a purchase in order to obtain a use-value, the person he purchases from undergoes the first phase, C-M. The metamorphosis of a commodity consists of a combination of opposites: C-M and M-C. The two phases together constitute a circular movement or circuit, C-M-C. The circuit of a commodity implies the existence of other circuits; the total of all of these different circuits constitutes the circulation of commodities.

The circulation of commodities leads to the rupture of bonds of a local and personal nature and thus permits exchange to develop beyond its apparent limits. There is a concurrent development of social relations of exchange that are entirely beyond the control of the conscious participants. Circulation is not extinguished with the consumption of a use-value, because money is constantly ejected to attract new commodities.

While C-M-C is a circuit, money does not describe a circuit, but is continually moving away from its source. The movement of money, called its currency, is an expression of the circulation of commodities. Commodities drop out of circulation as they are consumed as use-values. Money, in contrast, is continually present and necessary. If all commodities were to be purchased at once, the amount of money required to bring about their circulation would be equal to the sum of the prices of these commodities. The value of gold given, variations in the amount of money required are determined by the prices of commodities. However, as we have seen, money serves to separate sale and purchase. As transactions become spread over time, the same money can function as a means of circulation for a range of commodities. Thus, the amount of money required for circulation is equal to the total prices of commodities to be exchanged in a given interval of time divided by the number of moves or turnovers made by money in that time period. The velocity of the turnover of money reflects the rapidity with which commodities change their form.

Money becomes coin as a result of its function as the circulation medium. Coinage immediately develops a symbolic function as the representation of value and this function provides the basis for the development of paper money. By paper money,

Marx means here paper functioning as money, not credit money or bills of exchange. Therefore, paper money takes the place of gold as the circulating medium and is subject to the laws that control gold.

SECTION 3. MONEY

Money is the name given to the commodity that functions as a measure of value and as the medium of circulation. If the circulation of commodities is interrupted, then money becomes a hoard or store of value. Hoarding serves the social function of permitting changes in the money supply as the amount of money needed for circulation of commodities fluctuates.

It is the nature of exchange that money will be required as a means of payment as soon as there is a separation of purchase and sale. From here it is possible to separate payment and purchase. Credit money can be said to spring from the function of money as a means of payment. There develops a chain of payments in which each debtor's fulfillment of his obligations allows his creditors to fulfill their obligations in turn. The possibility of economic crisis is increased and its magnitude is amplified as a result of the development of credit. Marx pursues this theme at length later in *Capital*.

In the world market, money returns to its original form, gold bullion. It is here that gold achieves full recognition as the incarnation of social labour in the abstract. The central function of money in the international arena is as a means of payment permitting the settlement of accounts. Reserves are required for fluctuations in the world markets, so that changes in the balance of trade of a country can be adjusted through the transfer of gold bullion.

GLOSSARY

The following glossary compiles brief definitions of the central theoretical terms employed by Marx in Volume I of *Capital*. Many of these terms are used in various senses and with diverse shades of meaning. Indeed, the use and meaning of a term such as 'capital' or 'value' develop throughout the course of the text. We hope, therefore, that the reader will both find this glossary useful and be aware of its limitations.

absolute surplus-value: surplus-value produced by extending the length of the working day beyond necessary labour time and thus directly augmenting surplus labour time.

abstract labour: labour in its general or quantitative aspect as a producer of value, abstracted from its particular qualities as labour productive of a certain kind of use-values.

capital: value capable of self-expansion through the purchase and use of labour-power (a social relation) and the consequent production of surplus-value.

capital accumulation: the reinvestment (or capitalization) of a portion of surplus-value in new elements of constant and variable capital, thereby increasing the scale of production; also termed 'extended reproduction' and 'concentration of capital.'

centralization of capital: combination of individual capitals to form larger capitals as, e.g., in mergers and takeovers.

collective labourer: a cooperative combination of workers, e.g., necessitated by capitalism's socialization of the labour process; under capitalism, the collective labourer includes all those agents who perform productive labour for capital including intellectual workers in the sphere of production.

commodity: a product of human labour which is produced in order to be exchanged.

composition of capital: the division of capital into that part which purchases material means of production (constant capital) and that part which purchases labour-power (variable capital); in terms of use-values: the 'technical composition of capital'; in value terms: the 'value composition of capital'; the term 'organic composition of capital' expresses the dependence of the value composition on the technical composition.

concrete labour: labour as work of particular sort; labour as a creator of use-values; labour in its qualitative aspect.

constant capital: that part of capital which purchases material means of production (raw materials, auxiliary materials, and instruments of labour); that part of advanced capital which does not expand its value in production.

exchange-value: the relative proportions in which commodities exchange for each other on the market; an expression of their value or the form in which value is manifested.

fetishism of commodities: the mistaken idea that the value of a commodity is an intrinsic property of the commodity as an object; the failure to understand how exchange relations are determined by social relations.

forces of production: include the technical division of labour, the means of production, and the knowledge and skills available to the producers; the forces of production combine with the relations of production to provide the basis for a mode of production.

intensity of labour: the degree of effort expended in work; labour more intense than average creates more use-values, and hence more value than average in a given time.

labour-power: literally, the capacity for work; the commodity the labourer sells to the capitalist in exchange for wages; the use-value of labour-power is labour; its value is the value of the commodities comprising the worker's subsistence.

labour process: the process of creating use-values; its factors include the activity of the worker, the instruments of labour, and the subject of labour.

manufacture: that mode of production based upon a detailed division of handicraft labour within the workplace; entails the 'formal subjection' (social subordination) of labour to capital without fundamentally altering the technical basis of production.

means of production: the material factors of the labour process, including raw materials, auxiliary materials, and instruments of labour (broadly construed).

mode of production: literally, 'a way of producing,' used by Marx in several senses; the strongest sense is the one that combines forces and relations of production; each mode of production (e.g., the capitalist mode of production) represents a combination of a fundamental class relation, labour process, and form of extraction of surplus labour.

modern industry: that mode of production, specific to capitalism, which affects not only the social organization of production, but revolutionizes as well, its technical basis and, in so doing, results in the 'real subjection' of labour to capital.

money: a commodity (typically, gold or other precious metal) which serves as a universal value equivalent and consequently as the measure of value and the medium of commodity circulation.

necessary labour: that part of the working day during which the labourer produces value equal to the value of his labour-power, value that he realizes in his wage.

price: the expression of value in money; sometimes: the actual exchange proportions of commodities which may depart from their values (e.g., because of supply and demand).

primitive accumulation: the historical process of separating the independent commodity producer from the means of production; this separation ensures the existence of wage labour and therefore is a fundamental condition of capitalist production; additionally, all accumulation from outside the capitalist mode of production may be seen as primitive accumulation.

productive labour: under capitalism, labour which produces surplus-value for capital.

productivity (productiveness): the quantity of use-values of a particular sort produced in a certain amount of labour time; thus the value of commodities varies inversely with the average social productivity of the labour which creates them.

relations of production: the class relations necessitated by a particular mode of production; every mode of production combines forces and social relations of production; in the capitalist mode of production, the fundamental relation of production is the wage relation between the capitalist class and the working class.

relative surplus population: working-class population in excess of the needs of capital; serves to regulate wages through the supply of and demand for labour.

relative surplus-value: surplus-value produced as a consequence of shortening necessary labour time, for example, by decreasing the value of subsistence goods.

revenue: that portion of surplus-value which the capitalist spends for his personal consumption.

simple commodity production: the unity of the labour process and the process of creating value; differentiated from capitalist production of commodities in that it is undertaken by independent commodity producers who exchange the products of their labour rather than their labour-power: the basis for the development of surplus-value, wage labour, is absent.

simple reproduction: the expenditure of all of surplus-value as revenue so that there is no capital accumulation.

socially necessary labour time: the average amount of labour expended in the production of a commodity under current conditions (including, for example, the average productivity and intensity of labour).

surplus labour: that part of the working day extending beyond necessary labour; the time during which the worker produces surplus-value for the capitalist.

surplus-value: value accruing to the capitalist as a consequence of the working day extending beyond necessary labour time; the rate of surplus-value, the ratio of surplus-value to variable capital (wages) or of surplus to necessary labour time, expresses the degree of exploitation of labour by capital.

use-value: the use(s) to which a commodity may be put; its utility based upon its concrete properties as an object.

value: the amount of socially necessary labour time for the production of a commodity incorporated in that commodity.

variable capital: that portion of capital expended (in wages) for the purchase of labour-power; that part of advanced capital which expands its value in production.

wage: the value of labour-power in money, expressed on the surface of society as the price of labour; in real terms, the sum of commodities comprising the labourer's subsistence.

QUESTIONS

Chapter I, Section 1 and 2

1.1 Distinguish among use-value, exchange-value, and value.
1.2 Distinguish between abstract labour and concrete labour.

Chapter IV

4.1 What are the inherent limits of the simple circulation of commodities? Of the circulation of money as capital?
4.2 What are the objective bases of the circuits C-M-C and M-C-M? What is the subjective aim associated with each of these circuits?

Chapter V

5.1 What are the contradictions in the formula of capital?
5.2 Why can't the circulation of capital be a source of surplus-value?
5.3 What basic error lies behind the attempts to represent the circulation of commodities as a source of surplus-value?

Chapter VI

6.1 Why does Marx say that the value of labour-power includes a historical and moral factor? What determines the value of labour-power?
6.2 What conditions are required for the buying and selling of labour-power to become a generalized social process?
6.3 What are the peculiarities of labour-power as a commodity?
6.4 Why does Marx distinguish between labour and labour-power?
6.5 Drawing upon the material in Chapters IV to VI, explain how money, a store of value, becomes capital-value which is capable of self-expansion. What is capital?

Chapter VII
Section 1

7.1 Why does Marx associate the labour process with the production of use-values? What are the elementary factors of the labour process?
7.2 What characteristics are specific to the capitalistic labour process?

Section 2

7.3 How is the value of a commodity determined?

7.4 Demonstrate how the difference between the use-value and the value of the commodity labour-power results in the creation of surplus-value. Use a specific example.

7.5 In Marx's example, how does the spindle show up as a constituent part of a certain length of yarn, although the yarn does not contain a particle of steel?

7.6 Explain the meaning of the following passage: "We now see that the difference between labour . . . capitalist production of commodities." (p. 191)

Chapter VIII

8.1 What are constant and variable capital? Why does Marx use the terms 'constant' and 'variable'?

8.2 How is the distinction between concrete and abstract labour related to the distinction between constant and variable capital?

Chapter IX

9.1 The following are hypothetical examples meant to help concretize your understanding of the relations among the terms in Marx's theory:

(a) Suppose that a capitalist invests $20,000 in constant capital and $10,000 in variable capital. If the rate of surplus-value is 50%, and assuming that all constant capital is used up in production, what is the total value of the commodities produced?

(b) If a capitalist invests $3,000 in constant capital, $4,000 in variable capital and if his workers produce commodities worth $8,000, what is the rate of surplus-value? If the working day is of 12 hours duration, express the rate of surplus-value in terms of time.

9.2 Define necessary labour time and surplus labour time.

9.3 What errors did Nassau Senior make in his analysis of profit?

Chapter X

10.1 Work through the following examples:

(a) If the rate of surplus-value is 200% and necessary labour time is four hours, what is the length of the working day?

(b) Suppose that necessary labour time is six hours and that the working day is 12 hours long. If, as a result of the class struggle, the working day is reduced to nine hours, by how much is the rate of surplus-value changed?

10.2 Why is legislation regulating the length of the working day in

England divisible into two distinct periods? What is the nature of this division?

10.3 What are the two 'rights' involved in the struggle over the length of the working day?

10.4 Summarize Marx's account of the passage of the Factory Acts.

Chapter XI

11.1 What is the relation between the rate and mass of surplus-value?

11.2 What factors determine the minimal capital required for investment in a particular sphere of production?

Chapter XII

12.1 Distinguish between absolute and relative surplus-value.

12.2 Marx begins Part IV with "The Concept of Relative Surplus-Value" and then proceeds with chapters on "Cooperation," "Division of Labour," etc. Does this sequence tell us anything about his method of presentation?

12.3 Why are individual capitalists motivated to increase worker productivity through innovation?

12.4 Suppose that a capitalist invests $6,000 in constant capital and $3,000 in variable capital at a rate of surplus-value of 100% to produce 1,200 articles each valued at $10. Now imagine that, with the same investment in constant and variable capital, the capitalist doubles the productivity of his workers: (a) What is the social value of the new products? (b) What is their individual value? (c) If the products sell at their social value, what would the new rate of surplus-value be? (d) Would the products sell at their social value? (e) What happens when this productivity increase is generalized throughout the industry?

12.5 What is the relation between the value of a worker's labour-power and his productivity? How does this relation enter into the formation of relative surplus-value?

Chapter XIII

13.1 What does Marx mean by the term 'simple cooperation'?

13.2 Explain how simple cooperation results in an increase of relative surplus-value?

13.3 What are the two different aspects of capitalist control over production and from what do they arise?

13.4 Why is it that increases in productivity due to cooperation appear to be a function of capital?

Chapter XIV

14.1 In what ways does manufacture develop relative surplus-value?
14.2 How does the technical character of manufacture cause the minimum amount of capital which must be in the hands of each capitalist to rise?
14.3 What obstacles prevented the full development of the peculiar tendencies of manufacture?
14.4 How does the division of labour in manufacture make the worker a mere fragment of his own body?
14.5 Contrast the division of labour in society with the division of labour in a factory. What is the effect of the growth of the manufacturing division of labour on the social division of labour?

Chapter XV

15.1 Why does the title page "Capitalist Production" precede Chapter XV?
15.2 In this chapter, Marx describes a new mode of production in the development of capitalism and indicates the implications of this change. By utilizing the section headings, sketch an outline of the social and economic changes resulting from the transition from manufacture to modern industry.

Section 1

15.3 Explain how the simple cooperation of manufacture reappears in the factory and how the division of labour of manufacture reappears on a higher plane in the factory.

Section 2

15.4 What considerations limit the use of machinery in capitalism?
15.5 Distinguish between the value of machinery and the value transferred by machinery to the product.
15.6 What is the inherent contradiction in the use of machinery for the production of relative surplus-value? How is this contradiction manifested?

Section 3

15.7 What is the nature of the distinction between increased productivity and increased intensity of labour?
15.8 How is labour intensified? Does an increase in the intensity of labour: cheapen commodities; increase the rate of surplus-value; increase the mass of surplus-value?

Section 4

15.9 Drawing on material in Part IV, trace the separation of the intellectual powers of production from manual labour in simple cooperation through the development of manufacture to modern machine industry.

15.10 Explain why it is that the inversion of the instruments of labour acquires technical and palpable reality for the first time in the factory system.

Section 6

15.11 Why does Marx criticize the theory of compensation?

Chapter XVI

16.1 What is meant by the expression, "a specifically capitalist mode of production"?

16.2 How does capitalism impart specificity to the concept of productive labour and how is this concept changed as capitalism develops?

16.3 What is the difference between the formal and the real subjection (subordination) of labour to capital?

Chapter XVII

17.1 How do the length of the working day, the intensity of labour, and the productiveness of labour determine surplus-value and the value of labour-power?

Chapter XVIII

18.1 Why is it crucial to distinguish the rate of surplus-value (s/v) from the ratio of surplus-value to value created (s/v+s)?

Chapter XIX

19.1 Once again, Marx makes a distinction between essence and appearance and relates this distinction to a concept of science. Develop, as much as possible, Marx's concept of science on the basis of the following sections:
(a) "It is not our intention . . . perceptible by the senses." (p. 300)
(b) "In the expression 'value of labour,' . . . except Political Economy." (p. 503)
(c) "Hence, we may understand . . . of the vulgar economists." (pp. 505-506)

19.2 What was the dilemma of classical political economy relating to the theory of wages? How did Smith and Ricardo try to solve the contradiction? What is Marx's solution?

19.3 Give the principal reasons for the surface appearance and prevailing concept that wages are the price of labour. Compare the forms of exploitation in slave, feudal and bourgeois societies and the manner in which each conceals or reveals exploitation.

Chapter XX

20.1 What is the relation between the price of labour and the value of labour-power? Why does Marx use the term 'price of labour' rather than 'value of labour'?

Chapter XXI

21.1 Why is piecework so suitable to the capitalist mode of production?

Chapter XXII

22.1 What is the purpose served by this chapter? Why does it appear at this point in the text?
22.2 What are the consequences of international variations in the productivity and intensity of labour?

Chapter XXIII

23.1 How does our knowledge that capitalism is a system which reproduces itself allow us better to understand capitalist production?
23.2 What does Marx mean by 'simple reproduction'?

Chapter XXIV

24.1 Describe how capital is created out of capital. What makes extended reproduction (capital accumulation) possible?
24.2 Why is the exchange relation between capital and labour a mere semblance, foreign to the real nature of the transaction?
24.3 How can the capitalist increase accumulation without altering his own consumption?
24.4 Explain the concept of the labour fund and demonstrate its inadequacy for understanding the relative magnitudes of profits and wages.

Chapter XXV

25.1 What is the general law of capitalist accumulation?

Section 1

25.2 What are the value composition and the technical composition of capital? How do these relate to the organic composition of capital?

25.3 Why does Marx examine the unreal situation of an unchanging organic composition of capital? What is the cycle described by wages in the situation of an unchanging organic composition?

Section 2

25.4 Why does the technical composition of capital undergo a greater change than the value composition as capitalism develops?

25.5 How is the development of the social productivity of labour the most powerful lever of accumulation?

25.6 Distinguish between centralization and concentration of capital.

Section 3

25.7 Explain how the development of the social productivity of labour affects employment.

25.8 How do Malthus and his followers confuse the laws which regulate the general movement of wages with the laws which distribute the working population over different spheres of production?

Section 4

25.9 What is the relative surplus population? What different forms does this surplus population take?

Section 5

25.10 Does the remainder of this chapter support a theory of increasing impoverishment of the working class in material terms?

Chapter XXVI and XXVII

26.1 What does 'primitive accumulation' refer to?

26.2 How did the expropriation of the agricultural population create the preconditions for capitalistic wealth?

Chapter XXVIII

28.1 Why was legislation a necessary condition of capitalism in the early period of its development?

Chapter XXIX and XXXI

29.1 Describe the different processes and tempos of development of capital in agriculture and industry.

Chapter XXX

30.1 How did the separation of agrarian producers from their means of production affect the development of manufacturing?
30.2 What does it mean to say that means of subsistence were transformed into material elements of variable capital?

Chapter XXXII

32.1 What is the historical tendency of capitalist accumulation?
32.2 How did the petty mode of production further the process of capitalist development?

Chapter XXXIII

33.1 How did Wakefield propose to bring about capitalist development in the colonies?
33.2 What role does this last chapter play in Marx's exposition?

Chapter I
Section 1

1.1 Explain why, in capitalist society, use-values are the material repositories of exchange-value.
1.2 Distinguish between value and exchange-value.
1.3 Are value and use-value indissolubly connected? Can either exist in a commodity without the other?
1.4 Explain the word 'socially' in the term 'socially necessary labour time.'

Section 2

1.5 What are the two aspects of labour? Is there a contradiction between the two aspects?
1.6 Why is the division of labour prerequisite to commodity production? Does every social division of labour result in commodity production?
1.7 Can there be an increase in material wealth while the magnitude of value decreases?

Section 3

1.8 What are the various forms of value that Marx considers here? Why does he term exchange-value 'the form of value'?

Section 4

1.9 Why does Marx say that, "the relations connecting the labour of one individual with that of the rest appear, not as direct social relations between individuals at work, but as what they really are, material relations between persons and social relations between things." (p. 78) Has he not been arguing that this is only the appearance concealing the reality of social relations between persons?

1.10 Explain the nature of the relationship between social relations and labour in feudal society, capitalist society, and socialist society.

1.11 What is the fetishism of commodities and what is the origin of the fetish?

Chapter II

2.1 Why does the exchange of use-values develop into the exchange of products of labour as values, and why must commodities be realized as values before they are realized as use-values?

2.2 What are the steps in the conversion of products of labour into commodities? At what point in this process does the fetishism arise and how does it first manifest itself?

2.3 What did Marx mean when he wrote: "But one and the same set of transactions cannot be simultaneously for all owners of commodities both exclusively private and exclusively social and general." (p. 90) How is exchange obstructed by this contradiction? How was the contradiction resolved in practice?

Chapter III

3.1 What relation is expressed by the magnitude of value?

3.2 What is the relationship between price and value?

3.3 What are the different functions that money performs?
